The Beat of a Different Drum

THE BEAT OF A DIFFERENT DRUM

More stories from
The Hunter-Gatherer Way

Ffyona Campbell

Wild Publishing

First published in Great Britain by Wild Food Publishing in 2017.

ISBN 978-0-9575408-1-1

Printed and bound in Great Britain by Shortrun Press Ltd, Exeter

For my daughter

Elsa

spirited, strong, beautiful and kind

I am so proud of you

.

ABOUT THE AUTHOR

Ffyona Campbell was born in Totnes, Devon, in 1967. She spent many years exploring the world on foot and learning from Australian Aborigines, African Bushmen, Pygmies, and North American Indians. In 1997 she returned home to learn the wild food of her native land and to find out what had happened to us, 4,000 years ago, to turn us away from the hunter-gatherer life we loved. Since then she has pieced together what must have been an annual migration route we took as hunter-gatherers and has taught over 3,000 people how to identify wild food here in Britain through her day courses and her Year Long Wild Food course.

By the same author

Feet of Clay, a walk across Australia (Orion)
On Foot Through Africa, a walk the length of Africa (Orion)
The Whole Story, a walk around the world (Orion)
The Hunter-Gatherer Way, Putting back the apple (Wild)

ACKNOWLEDGEMENTS

When I wrote "The Hunter-Gatherer Way" it didn't feel right to mention one of my earliest teachers because he's so famous now and I wanted the work to be judged on its own merits. But when, in his autobiography "My Outdoor Life", Ray Mears wrote that the time he'd spent with me on my walk through Africa had helped to make him the man he has become, I felt it would be alright to acknowledge him now for the similar effect he'd had on me. So, thank you Raymond.

I would like to thank Martyn Forrester for coming up with this title 25 years ago. It was originally proposed for my book about the Africa walk, but the publisher had preferred "On Foot Through Africa". Being my own publisher now, I get to use it at last. So, thanks Mart, one instinctively does.

I would like to send love and gratitude to my dear friend Miranda Day for reading the first five chapters, helping to correct the grammar and spelling and, when I was so exhausted near the end of writing, greeting me with the news that it was "thrilling!" I can't tell you what that meant to me. And love and gratitude to my dear friends Mary Maguire and Anne Wright for all we've shared through the journey of our friendships over the years.

But most of all, unfailing in her support with her delightful wit and her constant love, my beautiful, feisty, intelligent, resourceful and carefree daughter, Elsa, my greatest teacher.

AUTHOR'S NOTE

The first book in this series, "The Hunter-Gatherer Way", was the culmination of 15 years of magical experiences in Nature and when I put them all together they seemed to reveal an incredible discovery to me.

As the manuscript went to print, nobody else had read it and so I had no idea whether it would have the same effect on anyone but me. Then the responses started to come in, like this one from a reader, Christopher Lane:

"I first started reading it on the living room floor, but after a few pages I think I knew my mind was preparing to be a little blown and I desperately didn't want anyone to disturb me! I ran upstairs to a quiet room, curled up and carried on, accompanied by slaps to the forehead and a childish kind of giggle....joy, something....at the sheer sense in what you were saying."

It was such an exciting feeling for me to read this, and the hundreds of reviews that followed from nearly 20 countries, because it was surely undeniable now: the magic I'd felt really *must* be there and the discoveries I'd made could very well be true.

Your comments encouraged me to continue sharing my journeys and so this second book is a continuation of exploring the mysteries that cross my path. By asking questions and putting things together from the answers I find, I see if they will make sense. Whilst the first book was explored through my experiences of visiting places and looking things up in libraries, it has saved me years of work to be able to ask questions and find answers by looking them up on the internet. The internet was a resource I just didn't have back then and without the use of it for this book I would probably still be saving up to visit many of the places which might have led me to the next step.

The subjects I cover here are just as they occurred to me. They fit with those I wrote about in "The Hunter-Gatherer Way" so it would be a good idea to read that book first.

Some people make sense of the world by taking things apart but for me I like making sense of it by putting things *together*. A bit like having a giant, incomplete jigsaw puzzle on my kitchen table and each experience I have is a piece which will fit somewhere into this puzzle. I believe that the pictures that begin to emerge reveal the truths behind life's mysteries.

To me the process of finding the pieces is sometimes like panning for gold; sifting through the day's observations until I notice something that lights me up. Then there's another feeling I get when a piece of information just doesn't make sense on its own. It's as though this thing is standing proud on the path and it catches my foot so that I trip and have to ask "What *are* you?" And then I just have to start hunting about for something that fits with it so that it *does* make sense. It won't lie down until I can find a place for it to fit into, a place where it belongs.

But sometimes I'm quite slow about it, sometimes it's been catching at my foot for years but I haven't paid any attention until one day something else falls into place that allows me to notice it. Or, it just gets so damn big I can't do anything but fall flat on my face in astonishment.

If I come up against a wall and give up I am denying myself the adventure of finding out what's on the other side. The connections I make might be different to those that you would make, but what's important is that I continue exploring and putting pieces together until something makes so much sense to *me* that it creates a door.

I hope these stories help your own thinking to run freely with the fluidity needed to see through the conditioning that has created walls between us and our understanding of Nature. Magic exists on the other side of those walls and you'll know it when you find it because it will make perfect sense to *you*. There are pages at the back for your notes.

The DRUMS

CHAPTER 1

Teaching people about wild food is a magical experience for me. Within just a couple of hours I see them transform from people who don't know how to find food but sense there must be something there, to people who are lit up like Christmas trees surrounded by presents.

But it's when I take them to the seashore in the summer and teach them about edible seaweed that the magic really takes hold of them. Here they become so engrossed in hunting amongst the rocks that they just don't hear me when I'm calling them back to the shore.

Watching the seaweeds swaying to and fro in the rising and falling of the waves creates a kind of hypnosis. The sparkles of sunlight glisten in mesmerising shimmers creating holograms on the burnished leather-like belts of the Kelp; the rock pools turn into cauldrons of sea jewels; the salty ocean air feels so enlivening and yet so dreamy, all at the same time. And they are lost to it.

I've seen this happen so many times that I've come to call it "the enchantment at the edge of the sea". It's so powerful that it can lull even the most sensible of people into feeling safe out there, despite the turning of the tide, until I can convince them to come back.

It never occurred to me that this phenomenon might actually be flagging up something extraordinary. Or that other pieces in this landscape might actually fit together with it, creating a whole picture which makes perfect sense. Until one day, the pieces became so overwhelming that a bigger picture was simply impossible to ignore. And with one final piece I realised I'd solved a puzzle I hadn't even noticed was there.

But, the journey to this realisation came very gradually, adding up with one unexpected experience at a time.

In British culture we have virtually nothing positive to say about seaweed despite having some of the best in the world and a total coastline of nearly 20,000 miles. Yet from the very first experience I had I realised our commonly held beliefs about it bear no relation to reality at all, as so often happens when we have been separated from something which was once very special to us.

Instead of being slimy, smelly and tasting pretty bad, seaweeds actually have flavours ranging from salty hazelnuts to smoky bacon; many are *dry* in the mouth, and none of them smell when they are cut freshly from the rocks.

The more seaweed I ate the more energy I had. Even without eating any carbohydrates, the energy from seaweed was so strong it felt as though I had the power of the sea simply coursing through my veins. I was thinking more clearly too, as though the sea was pushing its way through the mental debris in my mind, clearing channels, unrelenting in its push.

And it wasn't just me who was getting these remarkable feelings of mental activity. I gave some to a friend who was writing a final piece for her degree and after eating some Laverbread (boiled Laver seaweed) she was amazed to find she could think clearly for hours and hours through the night where she hadn't been able to before. Another friend, a creative genius at my daughter's school, ate the seaweed for supper and found that he couldn't sleep, his mind felt so alive and wanting to create. In the morning his wife came down to find he had written a whole new play in the night.

And it's not just the powerful energy or mental creativity which seaweeds give us which is so astonishing. There is a gel in seaweed which prevents it from drying out in the sun and I have seen this gel behave as though it is completely compatible with our skin. I've seen it relieve burns, not just a bit of sunburn on people who have come on my seaweed walks and forgotten their suntan cream, but a massive burn from boiling water. A baby's forearm had been scalded by a cup of tea, a blister had formed and had burst and he was screaming. Someone had come running to my tent asking for Aloe Vera. I ran back with a length of Kelp seaweed and wrapped the baby's arm with it.

The doctor who saw the baby in the local hospital said the Kelp had kept the wound cool and, unlike modern dressings, hadn't heated up with the heat of the wound. It had kept the wound moist; it had kept it sterile; and the iodine had begun to heal it. The Kelp had also calmed the baby, as soon as I had put it on he had stopped screaming, just soft tears falling. The doctor said that the seaweed was the *perfect* dressing.

So, as well as giving us huge amounts of energy and clarity of thought, the seaweed is also perfect for healing skin wounds.

I noticed more of its extraordinary abilities when I set up a seaweed stall at a farmers market 50 miles from the sea, in the Republic of Ireland. The towns people hadn't seen seaweed for sale for years but they remembered what their grandparents had used it for.

One way was to rub boiled Carrageen Moss seaweed into their hair to make it soft and shiny so I sold little packets of it as a home spa treatment. A woman came back to the stall saying that not only had it made her hair super soft and shiny, it had also healed the psoriasis she had in her scalp. Nothing she had used previously had made any difference to it, not even steroid cream from the doctor at 110 Euro a tube.

Word got around about this and soon people were trying out the seaweed gel on everything from eczema to deep purple acne, from stubborn cold sores to athlete's foot (my father's). The seaweed gel was healing everything. Week after week people came back to me with incredible stories of how it was heavenly to smooth it onto inflamed skin and how it was healing it within days.

I'll never forget how it felt when a school teacher returned to the stall, his face now clear of the psoriasis which the previous week he'd admitted was very hard to cope with, and now he was radiant and free of it.

Or when a woman who had lost her hair to chemotherapy pulled off her wig and showed me the thatch of soft downy hair which had now grown back within a week of using the seaweed gel morning and night.

The people who came to my stall that winter were struggling not only with skin conditions or post chemo hair loss but also with the aftermath of the banking crisis. I wasn't expecting anyone to smile at me but the people who returned to the stall with their extraordinary stories about the seaweed were so lit up with it, it was as though the seaweed hadn't just healed their skin, it had lit the fire inside them again.

They said that the seaweed was reminding them of a time of plenty, long ago, when their grandparents had known how to gather it, and when their mothers had boiled it on the hob for soothing sore tummies; for healing chest infections; or had dried the red/brown seaweed into moreish snacks to munch on from a paper bag in their pocket.

Seeing the seaweed again in their town was a reminder of the powerful plants that grow all around their island like a ring of strength and protection that cannot be manipulated by banks or foreign investment. The seaweed belongs to them and to their heritage and it will always be there. It evoked a twinkle in their eye too, allowing them to reveal to me, in hushed and whispered tones, something of their ancient folklore. Despite being good Catholic members of the community, many would tell me about their true beliefs in magical beings within Nature and their eyes would dance with the fire inside them as they told me their stories.

The seaweed had enabled me to catch a glimpse of the magic that lies just beneath the surface.

Back in Britain that summer I came across yet more of seaweed's abilities. When I took a friend who was suffering from severe anorexia to the shore for the day, she lay in a sun warmed rock pool and she kept saying that she hadn't felt so deeply nourished in years. She was just *glowing* with delight in how lovely it felt. I later found out that seaweeds release their nutrients into warm water where our skin has the ability to extract those nutrients out of the water and release them into our bloodstream. It's a process which feels so good that a multi-million pound industry has developed around it in the form of Thalassotherapy - seaweed spas.

During the course of a couple of summers of teaching more people about seaweed, I came to know three couples who'd had difficulties in starting a family. I knew that two of the most important substances needed for conception: laminarian and fucoidan are found in massive doses in seaweeds. Seaweeds are at their best in the summer which is the same time as we are at our peak of our fertility. After eating the seaweed two of the three women conceived.

I was beginning to realise, from my own experience and from the experiences of people around me that seaweeds are far more powerful than any other wild foods. They give us energy without carbs; they enable us to think clearly and for longer periods of time; they soothe and heal all manner of skin conditions; they nourish our hair, making it shiny and making it grow; their nutrients can be absorbed out of the water and through our skin into our blood stream; and they can help us to conceive.

An incredible relationship between us and the seaweed was beginning to reveal itself and as I started exploring more deeply into its unique set of properties a whole picture began to come together.

Seaweeds were the very first plants to grow on Earth. They contain *all* the vitamins and minerals vital for health. They are the most *powerful* foods on Earth.

The iodine in seaweed is anti-biotic, anti-bacterial, anti-viral, anti-inflammatory, and anti-septic, no wonder the seaweed gel was helping all manner of skin conditions. Iodine is vital for our immune system. It raises our metabolism giving us energy. In order for mammals to grow hair they need iodine. Iodine in seaweed is not just available to us when we eat it but it's also atomised into the air by the action of the waves. So when we breath in the sea air we are absorbing iodine through our lungs and into our blood stream which is why we feel so well at the seashore. Like the other nutrients in seaweed, iodine is also 100% transdermal, meaning that it can pass through our skin and into our blood stream.

Seaweeds increase our melanin production helping our skin to tan and they contain anti-oxidants which help repair our skin after sun damage.

Not only can the seaweeds help the *skin*, they are also very high in calcium. There is ten times more calcium in seaweed than in cow's milk. In order to absorb calcium you must also have the right amount of sodium, potassium and magnesium eaten at the same time. Seaweed, unlike any other food, contains *exactly* the right balance of these nutrients which means we can absorb *huge* amounts of calcium when we eat seaweed.

The combination of electrolytes and chlorides in seaweed and seawater create healthy cell walls so that they are strong and permeable allowing toxins to come out and huge amounts of nutrients to go in. Seaweeds can rid the body of pollution and heavy metals.

Seaweeds contain substances which increase brain function. Vitamin B12 rarely found in a plant source is found in seaweed, it is important for blood flow to the brain and cognitive functions like language. Taurine in red seaweed is important for the developing brain.

Magnesium in seaweed is important for the ability to store new information in neural networks. Zinc in seaweed is important in the development of memory. Iodine improves information processing, fine motor skills and visual problem solving. And iodine is a necessary element for the development of the whole of the central nervous system - the central nervous system is made up of the brain and the spinal cord.

All of this began to alert me to the possibility that there might be something extraordinary going on here. And I think that logically, if you put it all together, it says only one thing: evolution.

There is a theory about the origin of life on the planet that it began in the sea, around warm thermal vents. Over time life evolved and the sea became full of all manner of sea creatures. Eventually there came what is described as "the biggest leap in evolution" and life came out of the sea. But nobody knows how it did it. Nobody knows *how* life came out of the sea.

I think that the answer is right here on the seashore. I think it makes perfect sense that if life did come out of the sea it did it by eating the seaweed.

If life came out of the sea, where would it do it? Straight up a cliff? Not likely. Onto shifting sands? Not likely either, too difficult to get a grip. What about around low rocks where there were channels and crevices and calm pools? Yes, much more likely. And this is exactly the place where seaweeds like to grow.

Why would sea creatures be there in those channels and pools in the first place? Hiding from predators? Maybe, but only for a short time unless there was something nice to eat to there. Is there anything nice to eat in the rocky shores? Yes, not only are there the most nutritious plants on Earth but there are also a multitude of crustaceans which are also incredibly high in nutrients. In fact, the rocky shore is so rich and so abundant in food that you could call it the finest feast on Earth.

And the sea creatures who dined there weren't just taking in nutrition through their stomachs but also though the largest organ on their body – their skin.

In order for a fish to evolve into a land creature it would need a lot of calcium to grow bones. Is there any calcium in seaweed? Yes, not only a huge amount of calcium but also the other three electrolytes needed, in *exactly* the right proportions, for creatures to absorb that calcium – sodium, magnesium and potassium. So, they *could* grow bones.

If sea creatures were moving about in shallow water, they'd need substances to protect their skin from exposure to the sun and substances to heal cuts from the rocks. The gel in seaweed which is also released into the water around the seaweed is completely compatible with skin, keeping it moist in the sun, repairing sun damage and healing any air-born infections.

As the backs of their heads broke the surface they were in danger of overheating in the sun and also of being seen by predators from above. The iodine in the seaweed enabled some creatures to grow hair which cooled the head and also camouflaged them because when hair is long it looks just like seaweed.

For evolution to take place quickly, lots of generations need to be born. Seaweeds are very high in the substances we need in order to conceive, as well as folic acid for the healthy growth of the unborn babies.

And the development of the brain, such an important part of coming out of the sea, came from the huge doses of nutrients in the seaweeds. In fact a new international analyses lead by Professor Ole G Mouristsen from the University of Southern Denmark, has identified that a diet rich in seaweed could have been responsible for the unprecedented growth in our brains 2.5 million years ago.

Then I found the following information from studies done at Tulane University which outline the extraordinary effects of iodine in biology and I had no doubt that if life did come out of the sea, iodine and all the nutrients that are in seaweed could have done it because there's a thousand times more iodine in seaweed than in land plants:

"Thyroid hormones support nearly every body system. In humans and other backboned animals, the iodine-containing hormones guarantee proper development of the brain, skeleton, and organs.

Almost all body functions carried out in nearly every tissue rely on thyroid hormones. Their actions and influence are so wide-ranging that vertebrates cannot live without them. Among other things, thyroid hormones specifically affect brain development; heart rate; lung function; blood function; bone growth; steroid hormone production and breakdown; sugar, fat, and protein breakdown; and some immune processes.

Whether alone or in concert with other hormones, the indispensable messengers regulate life-sustaining processes essential for normal growth, development, reproduction, and even behaviour.

Throughout life, thyroid hormones influence vertebrate energy demands by stimulating cells to burn more oxygen. A cell's oxygen use creates heat to moderate body temperature in warm-blooded animals and fuel metabolism.

Seasonal changes such as fur moulting in mammals or skin shedding by reptiles is directed by thyroid hormones. The hormones start hair growth in rodents, sheep, and other mammals."

But, I knew there was one final piece missing: how did gills turn into lungs? And then one day someone who came on a wild food walk told me a story that gave it to me. He said that during the Victorian era, there was a fashion for gentlemen to keep Salamanders in an aquarium in the study. Everyone thought that a Salamander was just an aquatic creature until one day someone accidently spilt some iodine in the water and the Salamander climbed out. Iodine is needed for Salamanders to become amphibians. So, if it could do it for them, why not for us?

I have seen drawings of a horrible looking amphibian which is supposed to be the life form that came out of the sea. But there were many kinds of creatures in the sea back then, why would only one of them come out? And if many of them came out why would they all look the same? I think it's more likely that *many* sea creatures ate the seaweed and many of them came out of the sea as whatever eating the seaweed turned them into.

Since then the sea levels have risen all over the world and as this would have taken place in what is now under the sea we haven't found the evidence for it yet. The "Cradle of Humankind" in South Africa is supposedly where humankind began but, as it says on it's website, it's only heralded as such because so many skeletons have been found there in the limestone caves. Hominids may well have lived all over the world, it's just that their remains are only found at sites where conditions allowed for the formation and preservation of fossils.

*

I went down to the low rocky Devonian shore on some of the oldest rocks in the world, looked into the water and tried to imagine what it might have felt like to go through the process of coming out of the sea.

As I looked I remembered a couple of lovely observations two of my students had made: Bernie Thomas had said how very stimulating she'd found the seaweed environment and yet how completely relaxing at the same time; and Tim Lawrence had said how much the seaweed had felt like it was massaging his skin as he bravely swam amongst it in the deep water. To these observations I added my own:

The waves moving us in and out of the seaweeds embrace, very sensual, while also being rocked, the most gentle of all the movements we know; just the kind of movement around us that would be needed when massive change is occurring. We like this, we *want* to be here. The feeling of being suddenly lifted up by the waves makes us laugh. Perhaps laughter was the first sound we ever made above the water. Like a baby getting used to the sea, us being lifted up and down in the water was getting us used to the air. This is the movement of the sea – it lifts things out of it and leaves them on the shore and withdraws. The lifting and rocking and laughing and lifting right out – how we had laughed! Maybe it was laughter as well as the iodine atomised in the air that developed our lungs. The rock pools are pools between the worlds of sea and land, they are places of change. Rocks pools being the warmest water, changes things more quickly. There is so much to eat amongst the rocks, it's like a buffet that's always open, if we could go in and out we could feed all the time at a bar of the richest nutrients on Earth. We were absorbing even more of it through our skin in the warm shallow water. So much food. What happens when we eat a lot of food to this day? We change shape. In the channels our fingers and thumbs developed to hold onto the side and to pick out crustaceans. Being pushed up the beach ahead of the tide, the sea pushes things out of it. Then retreats leaving them on the beach. We love the sea, we love the beach. We didn't crawl out of the sea, we were lifted out of it. We love drying out on the sand. Being by the sea we just want to sleep, lying out on the rocks or the soft sand. Even when we could walk we kept going back in and laughing and hunting in the pools and feasting because we love it still. I think this is the real cradle of humankind – the lifting up, the rocking, the learning to stand on the shore and dry out. When something is turning into a mammal in an aquatic environment there will be a stage when we are both and I don't think we all looked like that ugly lizard - it's not half mammal. Fresh water streams that come down to the sea cut through the rough rocks making them smooth: this is the easiest way into the sea and so the easiest way out of it. This is where we tasted sweet water for the first time and began to change into being able to drink it and then to follow it.

*

When I came home and told Elsa, my daughter, what I had found, she said:

"That's very interesting Mum. But if there's something that could change us from sea creatures into land creatures, is there also something there that can help us go back again?"

I thought for a moment and realised the question to ask would be "*Did* anything go back?" and Elsa said "Yes. Whales and dolphins. They have lungs and skeletons with arms and legs. They must have come out for a while and gone back in. Is there anything on the shore that could have helped them do that?"

I thought about it, I thought about how does change *actually* occur? How does it occur in *my* life? I was learning to play the guitar at the time; at first my fingers just wouldn't do what I wanted them to so why did I keep trying? Because even though I couldn't do it at first, I could feel a strong longing for something that was just out of my reach. I knew that if I just continued to push myself on through the discomfort of change whilst also being enveloped in what felt like a honey pool of encouragement by my teacher, I would be able to do it; I would be able to cast off the restriction of inability and run freely with in music. And so I was able to keep going and finally I was able to play something.

And I thought about how this would be on the seashore, if there was anything like that there? And I remembered how so many of the people I have taken out on a seaweed walk just couldn't come back in when I called them. How they were so entranced, so held in the magically hypnotic dance of sunlight and seaweeds as though they were totally spell bound within an enchanting embrace. Like a cocoon that holds a promise of an outcome if we just stay within its honeyed pools and feed on its luscious nutrition a little longer.

I think that this embrace, this enchantment at the edge of the sea, has been there for millions of years, enabling life to come out of it, and for life to go back in.

CHAPTER 2

One of the comments about "The Hunter-Gatherer Way" was a question about why I hadn't mentioned the Bronze Age. I had written about my views on the Stone Age and the Iron Age and how I'd felt that natural phenomena had been used by the clever elite to create a culture of fear so that others would work for them, enabling the clever ones to live a luxurious life without any drudgery.

The reason I hadn't mentioned the Bronze Age, the age which came after the Stone Age and before the Iron Age, was because I didn't have anything to say about it. I couldn't make sense of why people would go to all the trouble of smelting a substance like Bronze which wasn't as sharp as flint or as strong as stone. All it seemed to be good for was making ornamental things and as I'm not an ornamental type of person, I just couldn't see the point. I had forgotten my old saying that when something doesn't make any sense it's not a sign to turn away; instead it's a *flag* to start hunting about for pieces of information that must have become separated in our culture and if put together again would make a whole picture which would make perfect sense.

So, my journey into the Bronze Age began one day when I was walking up the hill from the rocky shore, a heavy basket of freshly cut seaweed in each hand, feeling rather pleased with myself for such a magnificent haul but also rather lonely and slightly bored. Elsa had gone away to Ireland for a few weeks and I'd done just about everything I like to do with my first few days of freedom. But now, as I looked ahead to the evening and I remembered that I was going home to an empty house, I was relieved to notice a poster attached to a lamppost: a talk was being given that very night about the Bronze Age.

So, I thought I'd go along and see if I could learn something about this old puzzle; this strange age which was so beautiful to behold and yet so seemingly useless. And as I laid out the seaweed to dry in the attic I started to get a sense that something big was coming; a big trip.

The talk was by an archaeologist about the recent extraordinary finds of a burial cist high up on Dartmoor at Whitehorse Hill. Nothing like this had ever been found on the moor before. The contents were unusually well preserved in the peat and so they had revealed a number of very important early Bronze Age artefacts. These items were shown to us, one slide at a time with an explanation as to how they showed the individual to have a very high status in the community. This is what they found:

In the bottom of the cist had been a layer of purple moor grass and meadowsweet flowers. Upon this was laid a unique textile garment made up of a double layer of finely-woven nettle fibres edged with piping and triangular appliqués of calfskin. The superb quality of the stitching, as well as the striking colour contrast of light and dark, implied that this was not an everyday sort of garment but probably a ceremonial one.

An animal pelt bundle was laid on top of the garment, it was found to have come from the back of a Black bear. Inside the pelt were the cremated remains of a person possibly aged between 15 and 25. The gender was unknown. It was believed to be a female only because of what they thought the artefacts were for which were found with the remains.

A copper-alloy pin was also found in the folds of the pelt and lying beside the fur bundle was a basket with a lid. The basket and its lid were made of lime bast which is made from the inner bark of the lime tree. I knew that it takes a huge amount of preparation to use lime bast, a lot more time and effort than anything else you can make a basket from. Around the top of the basket was a most striking decoration of light and dark stitching made with cow hair.

Inside this basket, and spilling out from it, were the following objects: a flake of flint; a tin bead; 7 amber beads; 92 shale beads; 109 clay beads; a narrow tightly woven band of cow hair inserted with 32 tiny tin studs placed at regular intervals along it; and two pairs of wooden studs made of Spindle wood.

The archaeologist then showed us a picture of what they thought all these artefacts had been used for and a photo of a model was flashed up on the screen: the fur pelt was draped around her shoulders, some of the beads hung on a necklace around her neck, the band of tin studs was on her arm and two of the wooden studs were in her earlobes.

Then he said that the archaeologist Alison Sheridan had remarked that amber and tin would produce a spark and she referred to this as "Supernatural jewellery".

I nearly fell off my chair. I could hardly believe what he'd just said. I could barely contain myself until question time to ask him what he'd meant by that. When finally the time came for questions the archaeologist explained that he'd meant you'd get an electrostatic charge off them.

"What does *electrostatic charge* mean?" I asked.

Without turning around, someone in the audience kindly explained: "It means static electricity." Nobody else seemed remotely interested in how extraordinary this was: Bronze Age people knowing about static electricity? That's not something I'd ever heard before.

I began to imagine what this might have looked like: the hair on the fur pelt standing up all around her shoulders and anyone who touched her getting an electric shock. What a power trick! Who was this person? And why, if this was really true, was she (or he) behaving like that? For fun? Was this a con trick? Why would that be? Suddenly the Bronze Age got very interesting indeed and I wanted to make sense of it.

As soon as I got home I looked up "Bronze Age and electricity" and found nothing. Then I tried "Bronze Age and static electricity", again I found nothing. This was a pretty major idea that Bronze Age people knew about static electricity and yet there was *nothing* about it. So, I would have to work it out for myself: did this Bronze Age person really know what they were doing with amber and tin to make static electricity? And if so, was it just known about up on Dartmoor? Was Dartmoor once a centre of such things or did it come from somewhere else? If so where? And what were they using it for? Who was this person in the burial cist and what were they saying with their power jewellery? Why had such a young person been given the grave status of royalty?

There were a lot of questions to answer.

So, I decided to start with what I thought was the most unusual item in the basket: the amber beads. I knew nothing about amber except from the large pendant I'd observed in my mother's jewellery box. As a child I had been very interested in the expression on the face of the dead insect caught inside it but I had never liked the feel of the pendant itself because it was always disappointingly warm, not cold as it looked like it ought to be. Years later when I'd wanted to know what prehistoric trees smelt like I had bought some small pieces of amber because I knew it was fossilized tree resin. I had pounded the pieces in a pestle and mortar, lit them in an incense burner and breathed in the scent. But I knew nothing else about it.

So, I went into a crystal shop in Totnes to get an education. I asked them what they could tell me about amber? They gave me a Care Card with instructions about "How to look after your piece of amber." It said you must be careful not to rub it because the surface would get pitted. It didn't say anything about an electrostatic charge so I asked the assistant if she'd heard anything about this? She said "All minerals and crystals give off some kind of charge because everything is energy isn't it? We are all energy...."

I knew there was a stall in the market square on a Friday which only sold amber. I wanted to talk to the woman who ran the stall and see what she could tell me but it was now only Tuesday and so I had to contend with finding out more online. I did an internet search about amber and found out that its Greek name is ilektron which is where the word "electricity" comes from. That's quite a coincidence.

When did the Greeks give it that name? I found out that the earliest written record of amber's ability to give off a static electric charge was made by an Egyptian-educated Greek, Thales of Miletus. Apparently, he was the first to discover that if you rub amber with animal fur it will attract lightweight objects like feathers and straw. His record of this was made about 600BC but the Bronze Age cist was made over a thousand years before that. Could it be that Thales, called the "Father of Philosophy" by Aristotle, was simply the first person to write it down and had therefore been accredited with it's discovery?

My next question was where does amber actually come from? Is it native to Britain? I knew that amber is a tree resin but which trees and where? I found out that much of the world's amber comes from vast forests of coniferous trees which edged what is now the Baltic sea. Their resins dropped into the salt water. Tons and tons and tons of it and, over the last 44 million years, environmental pressures fossilized the resin into the substance it is today. I found out that though it's not native to Britain it does sometimes get washed up on the east coast because it floats across from north western Europe. In fact, the way to tell if you have genuine amber is that it will float in seawater but if it's an imitation it will sink. People actually fish for it. In 2010, a Danish fisherman caught one of Denmark's largest pieces in his net: an amber rock weighing as much as a small person.

There are amber museums in Copenhagen and Gdansk showcasing the magnificent pieces that have been crafted over the years, and as I was exploring their websites I came across a reference to the Amber Road. Looking this up I found out that the Amber Road was an ancient trade route for the transfer of amber from northern Europe to Egypt.

The Egyptians and Greeks called amber "the gold of the north" and it was so important that the burial mask and the breast ornament of the pharaoh Tutankhamun contained large Baltic amber beads. That's quite a thing then for this young person up on Dartmoor to have seven amber beads in a basket.

By this time it was Friday and I went to visit the amber market stall in Totnes. The stall was loaded with amber necklaces, beads, pendants and bracelets. All I wanted were seven beads to experiment with so I asked the woman who ran the stall if she had any spares? She kindly brought out a small box and gave me one of the beads. "How many do you want?" she asked. "Seven." I said. "Oh no!" she said, "I can't sell you seven beads! Oh no, only one."

Why on Earth? This is a stall selling amber isn't it? I'm glad I remained open and receptive because she began to explain that these beads were very special to her. They had been specially made for her by an amber artist friend of hers as end pieces for necklaces. This once prolific artist was now unable to work due to failing health so, these individual beads were priceless to her now. I understood and realised that if I was to have my experiment I would need to select a small bracelet instead.

I wanted the beads to resemble those from the burial find but as I hadn't seen those beads for real (because they are in storage in a Plymouth museum awaiting the building of a new museum in which to house them) I could only guess at what they looked like from my memory of the photograph in the talk. There were hundreds to choose from so I took my time. Finally I selected one which seemed to have the kind of surfaces which I thought would increase the contact area when rubbing with an animal pelt.

I took the bracelet off the stand and presented it to the woman on the stall to indicate that I wanted to buy it. When she saw the one I'd picked her face went white and for a moment she couldn't speak. Crikey, I thought, I wonder what's wrong now?

"Of all the hundreds of bracelets on my stall," she finally said, "you have chosen the only one which was made by my friend's husband. He is also an amber artist. He once made a replica of a Bronze Age amber bracelet found in a burial chamber in Italy."

Bingo. I went home with my amber bracelet and rubbed the beads with sheepskin. Nothing happened. Then my dog walked past and I briskly rubbed the beads along her back and noticed her hairs begin to stand up. I then held the beads over some small pieces of paper and they began to stir. I wanted to do some more rubbing but it was only the back hairs which seemed to have this effect and with all the attention she was getting she just kept rolling over hoping I would rub her tummy instead. So, I had to leave the experiment for a while and take her by surprise another time.

In the meantime I turned my attention to the extraordinary thing the woman on the amber stall had said: the man who had made this bracelet had made another, a replica of one found in a burial chamber in Italy. So, there were more amber beads in Bronze Age burials in Europe. I started looking for more information about them.

There were several finds in Britain too, especially along the south coast of England, and as I read about each one, I kept coming across references to the amber beads being "well worn". The explanation given by archaeologists was that these would probably have been worn down because they were heirlooms. But surely if they were heirlooms they wouldn't be being buried at all? Heirlooms would be passed on to the next generation, just as they had been handed down to the person in the grave. I couldn't believe that none of these people had any descendants or relatives. More likely, I felt, the amber beads were well worn because they had been *rubbed*.

Because I couldn't see the original beads from the Whitehorse Hill find I tracked down the jeweller, Jamie Inglis, who had made replicas of the amber beads. We had a chat on the phone and I asked him to describe the surface of the original beads. He confirmed that they were indeed "very pitted".

I continued looking for information about other amber beads found at Bronze Age sites and I came across the website of an archaeological excavation at Must Farm in Peterborough which is still active. It was a Bronze Age settlement built on a platform over a river sometime between 1000 and 800BC. There had been a fire back then and it had burnt down so quickly the archaeologists had even found a bowl in the silt below the platform with the cereal and the spoon still in it.

I looked at the images of things they have discovered and saw the amber beads, dark and pitted. Then I saw a photo of a blue glass bead. I didn't know glass was made in the Bronze Age. So I contacted the archaeologists and asked where they thought the blue glass bead had come from? They kindly emailed me back to say they were quite sure it had come from Egypt. And it was likely to have come from the same glass makers who had made the blue glass in the head piece of the pharaoh Tutankhamun.

Excited by this I did a search to see if glass has electrostatic properties too and I found that it does: when amber is rubbed with animal fur it gives a positive charge and when glass is rubbed with silk it gives a negative charge. I looked up electrostatic experiments to see if there was anything about how to use amber and glass and found that *all* the early experiments to demonstrate an electrostatic charge used amber and glass.

So, what do they do?

When these two substances are charged up they will move towards each other without anyone touching them. They can make a tin can (or a tin bead) roll along a flat surface. They can make a lightweight object stick on a wall without anything holding it up. And if you pour water from a height, they can bend the stream to left and right. It's called the triboelectric effect.

As our young person on Dartmoor didn't have a blue glass bead in her basket but a lot of shale beads in the same flattened donut-like shape as the blue glass bead at Must Farm, I looked up to see if shale has electrical properties too. There were pages and pages on the subject of the "complex electrical properties of shale". I'm just guessing here, because I couldn't understand them, but I think it could be within the realms of possibility, that failing a blue glass bead, a shale bead would do. I also found that the blue glass beads in the flattened donut-like shape are used to this day: you will find them on the top of many telegraph poles between the wires and the pole, they are there to stop the electricity from arcing across to the pole because electricity can jump.

Making a demonstration of getting things to move without touching them or making things stick to a wall without anything holding them up would have looked like magic to people back in the Bronze Age. If you were able to do this you would have been thought of as a magician. And magicians can get people to do things for them.

Then I remembered, from my favourite book as a child called "The Ship that Flew" by Hilda Lewis, that Egyptians believed in magic.

It was time to check out the Pharaoh himself.

I knew nothing about King Tutankhamun except for his incredibly striking burial mask of blue and gold stripes. So I began to read up about him and his beliefs and found out that magic in ancient Egypt was considered *essential* for life. To the Egyptians, a world without magic was inconceivable. It was through magic that the world had been created, magic sustained the world daily, magic healed when one was sick, magic gave when one had nothing, and assured one of eternal life after death.

Sounds a bit like the promises of Christianity.

The Pharaoh had been given the name that meant he was the living image of Amun, the Sun God, and so his burial mask depicted the rays of the sun in the clear blue sky. Supporting their beliefs was a strong emphasis on the importance of metals reflecting the glory and power of the gods and the importance of aligning yourself with the gods because you needed to prepare yourself for going through judgements in the underworld after your death in order to live happily in the afterlife. A culture based on these kinds of beliefs is one which is very good at getting people to do things for it like build temples or fight wars or trade goods. Because who can argue with the idea of life after death? It must surely have been a special day for the elite when someone came up with that one and saw the effects it had on people.

Then somewhere during my research into the Amber Road trade route, I came across this ancient mythological story:

One day, Phaethon, the son of Helios, the God of the Sun, managed to convince his father to allow him to drive his horse-drawn sun chariot down the firmament. The father agreed but as soon as the horses felt that the driver was inexperienced, they bolted. The sun then burnt the African land to a desert and turned its inhabitants black. So as to prevent further damage, Zeus was forced to strike Phaethon with a lightning bolt into the River Eridanus. Phaethon's sisters, the Heliades, lamented his fate, cursing the Gods, so they were turned into amber-teared poplar trees. Grieving they kept crying and their tears became resin which turned into amber. Years later the sea is still throwing the sisters tears to the shore.

This story reminded me of something else that static electricity can do...

I looked up how to build up a static electric charge in your body and found an extraordinary video of a physics professor, Walter Lewin, demonstrating this phenomenon by "beating" one of his students with a pelt of cat fur.

(Youtube: Electric Charges and Forces, Coulomb's Law, Polarization at 22:40).

I'm quite sure the idea of beating someone with an animal fur pelt to build up an electrostatic charge wasn't thought up in a physics laboratory. More likely it was noticed much earlier in history when animal skins were being used all the time.

In the experiment, the student being beaten with the fur pelt is so charged with static electricity that when he holds a special rod he is able to make it glow in the dark. The rod is designed to show the large audience the amount of static electricity he has inside him.

Thinking back to our young magician on Dartmoor, I wouldn't think she would have beaten someone *else* with an animal fur pelt so they would have a lightning bolt coming from their finger tips. That would have been giving her power away. And having someone else beat her would be undignified. Then I remembered the dance of a witch-doctor I'd heard about in central Africa: she was jumping about beating herself with an animal pelt, shuffling her feet on the floor and getting herself into a trance.

So, if our young magician had beaten herself with an animal pelt whilst also doing a shuffling dance on a black bear skin rug, a good amount of static electricity would have built up in her. And if she had then touched the tin bead she would have produced a lightning bolt from her fingertip.

When I watched more videos of static electricity being demonstrated I noticed how often people would rub items on their shirt. I remembered the ceremonial cloth in the cist which had different kinds of fabrics in patches stitched strongly together and I thought how useful it would be to use such a thing to rub the different items on the different fabrics to charge them.

Professor Walter Lewin says in his lecture that in order to generate static electricity you need *dry* conditions. I thought about the lime bast basket, a very difficult and time consuming material to make a basket from. I looked up the special properties of lime bast and found that it has excellent water-repellent properties so it would have been perfect for keeping the beads inside very dry.

My feeling is this was not a necklace all the time but could have been used as individual beads which, when hung up individually and rubbed, could create an extraordinary display of magic. If you are able to make things move without touching them as well as having lightning bolts coming from your finger tips you're in business to get anything you want.

So, what *did* she want?

This was the Bronze Age, right? Who needed Bronze? Not us, we were a mixture of hunter-gatherers and Neolithic farmers.

So, who *needed* Bronze?

Egypt.

Egypt needed huge amounts of Bronze for making weapons and shields, for armour and cladding chariots, for erecting sculptures and honouring Gods. But the copper available to the Egyptians contained a lot of natural arsenic which meant it became spongy. Somewhere along the line it was found that adding tin to copper would strengthen it, lower the melting temperature, make a more fluid liquid to pour into the stone moulds and make a denser metal. This allowed for complex shapes and *longer* swords. It would be less likely to corrode and easier to sharpen and remain sharp.

Egypt had a supply of copper but it needed tin. But tin is a very rare metal. There's only 2 parts per million in the Earth's crust compared to copper which is 70 parts per million. And one of the largest natural deposits of tin in the whole of Europe is on Dartmoor.

Cassiterite, the name for tin oxide, forms in granite. Dartmoor is made of granite. It was so prolific in its production of tin that the British Isles were known to the Egyptians as the "Cassiterides", the "tin islands".

The tin bead and tin studs found in the burial cist on Dartmoor were the earliest known tin workings ever found in the south west. When I watched the BBC documentary, Mystery of the Moor, about the making of each of the elements of the find using methods which would have been used back then, the smelting of the tin was very interesting. The process begins with tin ore which is black. This is pounded to make a black powder which is then put into a stone crucible. The crucible is then placed in a fire. The fire is just an open fire like you'd have if you were camping except that it is being fuelled by bellows to make it super hot. After some time and the crucible is lifted out and the black powder has been transformed into a shining stream of silver.

The contrast of the black powder and the silver stream reminded me of the black and white stitching on the top of the lime bast basket; and the arrangement of light and dark fabrics on the garment; and the light and dark assembly of the necklace where the tin bead shone brightly beside the black of the clay beads; just as the tin studs were able to glisten brightly against the black horse hair on the armband. The colour scheme was exactly like the magical transformation of the tin.

Tin ore is very heavy and tends to sink in alluvial deposits in river beds having been washed down from the granite seams on the moor. Its dark colour makes it easy to see in the water. Trenches were dug so the lighter gravel was washed away and the heavier tin would sink. They made reservoirs and diverted streams. The valleys of south Devon were being searched and "streamed" over and over again.

It must have been pretty laborious work and so that the men continued to provide Egypt with this most valuable of metals, I think that the person whose remains were found in the cist at Whitehorse Hill was one of a whole lineage of people there with special knowledge to inspire the men to work. I think that she used demonstrations of magical displays with the set of beads to inspire the workers with awe and reverence, enchanting them and bewitching them, reassuring them of the riches to be had in the life hereafter and also maybe frightening them a bit too, as is the way of religion.

If you stand at the foot of the Dartmoor escarpment to this day and look up, everywhere you look along the skyline you will see the remains of man-made stone cairns. These cairns were made during the Bronze Age. They line the horizon like beads. Perhaps each one contains cremated remains and amber beads. The Valley of the Kings it may not be, but The Skyline of the Magicians could be just as powerful.

As the tin workers hunted for the black rocks and no doubt tired of it too, they need only look up and see the cairns on the skyline to be reminded of the power and the magic and the promises of a wonderful time in the afterlife if only they didn't abscond but continued in their work.

The motivation had to be very strong. Why else would anyone spend their days and years hunting about for bits of black rock in the mud when they could have been running wild and free like the hunter-gatherers who no doubt stood on the river banks and watched them, asking themselves the same question.

CHAPTER 3

Letting myself follow my logic and finding it led to a plausible answer about who might have owned the amber necklace and what they were doing with it, was immensely satisfying. It was like tracking an animal through the woods and finally finding it.

It feels so important to do this kind of exploring because every time I feel like I have shed light on a mystery, at least to my own satisfaction, it feels like I have removed one more brick from the wall of conditioning that is separating us from Nature. Even though we are not as caught up as we once were in the nonsense of a civilisation that has yoked us with promises of the life hereafter, we are still separated from Nature by beliefs which have been influenced by all the cultures we've had in this country for the last 4,000 years. Some of those cultures and belief systems we don't even know about but they have still left their mark on us.

So, with the satisfaction of the amber necklace journey still strong within me, and feeling the importance of continuing to expose the nonsense that has been left in our culture, I decided the time had come to turn my attention to a mystery that has been annoying me all my adult life: stone circles.

Stone circles were also made in the Bronze Age and nobody knows what they were for. So, it was going to be a tough mystery to crack especially as, unlike many of my friends, I've never really enjoyed visiting them. Apart from the annoying fact that I couldn't work them out, they always seemed so roughly done, so scruffy and haphazard and without the finesse of earlier times that I couldn't understand what all the fuss was about.

Even though I'd shared some of my ideas in "The Hunter-Gatherer Way" about what I'd felt was going on at Stonehenge, the reason for other kinds of stone circles had always eluded me. But, enough was enough, it was time to put an end to that annoyance and start exploring.

I know it has long been thought that ancient monuments are some kind of generators of energy because they often emit far higher levels of magnetic energy than the surrounding area which apparently gives visitors strange feelings. But I wanted to just open my mind and see what trail began to emerge. So, I let go of any pre-conceived ideas so that I could begin my own journey into this mystery.

I know that superstition comes into a culture at the time when hunter-gatherers are being turned into farmers. I learned about this process from a woman who had witnessed this first hand when she saw hunter-gatherers in the Amazon being turned into coffee farmers. I'd asked her what she saw change about them? She said their beliefs in the natural order of things became muddled and they became superstitious for the first time. They became afraid of silly things when before that they had been only confident and self-assured in the forest. Once they started asserting their dominance over the land by becoming coffee farmers things didn't make sense to them anymore, they were not as in control now, despite what they had been lead to believe, and so they became afraid and came up with nonsense to explain their fears.

I live in south Devon so Dartmoor is right on my doorstep. There are 17 stone circles on the moor. There are also over 5,000 *hut* circles, these are the remains of Bronze Age houses which aren't the same as stone circles. Apparently archaeologists rarely find anything remaining in the soil of a domestic nature in a stone circle, and so the general feeling is that they were of ceremonial use though nobody knows what that ceremony was. That's what I wanted to try and work out.

When I was exploring the trail of the amber necklace, I became alerted to the idea that some substances are more able to conduct electricity than others. Copper, for example, the main component of Bronze, is very good at conducting electricity and of course that's what we use it for to this day in all our electrical wiring. (I'm still wondering whether the copper alloy pin found in the fur pelt was somehow another instrument or prop in the Whitehorse Hill person's collection of things with which to make a magical electric display; especially as there was no evidence found that it was used to hold the pelt together.)

As I let my mind hover over the idea of a magical electrical display with the beads, I wondered whether this might just be a small scale version of what could have been done on a much bigger scale. We know that the moor was cleared of trees during the Bronze Age and people always say that it was for firewood but I'm not so sure. If the moor was cleared of trees it would be the perfect place for a large scale electrical display. Just as Stonehenge didn't begin as a giant monument but as a smaller version of itself first, to get it right, and then scaled up, so it might be here.

The stones of the stone circles are made of granite. So, I looked into whether granite is a good conductor of electricity and I found that it is: it's so good in fact that it frequently attracts lightning. In Yosemete

National Park in America, a granite peak called Half Dome favoured with local climbers is known locally as "a giant lightning rod".

When I looked into what happens when you are in a granite area when it is struck by lightning I found photos of people with their hair standing on end, it looks like they have a halo around their head.

(You can see one here: http://www.dailymail.co.uk/news/article-2381677/How-know-youre-struck-lightning-Picture-brothers-hair-end-minutes-before.html.)

The boys are smiling in the photo because they think it's funny that their hair is standing on end, they don't realise that these halos mean they have become positively charged and the negative charge in the sky above them will try to connect with them, turning them into a lightning bolt. They survived this but someone else near them did not.

In a book called "Outdoor Leadership" by John Graham, I also came across a more in depth account of what it's like to be in a lightning strike when the author and some friends had been climbing on Grand Teton, Wyoming. I looked up to see if it is made of granite: it is.

They had been climbing since early morning under clear blue skies when, just short of the summit, dark clouds began scudding directly over them.

"In five minutes the entire sky was dark and a wind that meant harm began to blow. A strange buzzing filled the air, like radio static. I looked over at Allen, who was pointing back at me. His hair was standing straight up. Small tongues of blue flame jumped from the tip of his ice axe.

"Get rid of metal!" yelled Steve behind me. He had climbed in these mountains before.

They threw their climbing hardware 20 feet away. Still, static buzzed in their ears, as if coming directly from their bodies.

"Hug the ground!" yelled Steve. "Get yourself as low as you can!"

Thunder now boomed all around us and the first flashes of lightning forked from the dark sky. We spread eagled ourselves in the snow. Hailstones the size of gumballs began pelting us, the bigger ones hitting with enough force to leave bruises. I began to shake uncontrollably from the cold. My parka was lying only a few feet away, on the rock where I'd left it. I raised my head and arm to grab it. "Don't!" yelled Steve.

It was too late. That small movement focused the electricity around me. I got my head down fast enough so that the bolt missed me and struck a large boulder 10 feet away. The rock was wrapped in fire, tongues of flame arcing in all directions. A thunderous boom rocked the mountain, deafening us.

Finally we gathered our wits, dug our equipment from under a blanket of hailstones and continued on to the top of the 'biggest lightning rod' for 200 miles in any direction.

To this day I can't see a lightning sky without remembering how that Teton rock looked, bathed in blue flame."

The images from this account seemed so biblical: the sudden darkening of the sky, the halo around their heads, the tongues of blue flame on a metal tool that didn't burn, the fear and the lying flat on their faces, and then the lightning bolt setting a massive boulder on fire. Superstition is made powerful by such realities.

I looked into whether Dartmoor gets struck by lightning a lot and found that it does. There is a study of lightning strikes in Earth's history called "Paleolightning" and Dartmoor is in a lightening belt.

Then I thought about how the greatest collection of stone circles and stone rows in the world is actually at a place called Carnac in Brittany, France. I checked to see if their stone circles are also made of granite and found that they are. In fact, they are made of exactly the same granite as Dartmoor because it was formed at the same time. Carnac is also in the lightning belt.

Carnac also has ancient tin mines and amber beads have also been found in some of its Bronze Age burial chambers.

I looked up to see if another famous place for stone circles, Orkney, has had any connection with lightning and found that one of the stones in the great Ring of Brodgar had been hit. There is a notice there which says: 'Visitor Information: This stone was struck by lightning on the 5th June 1980 causing it to shatter. Such events may also have occurred in earlier times, and might account for the damaged state of several other stones in the ring.'

Then I came across an eye witness account of lightning at a stone circle in Stanton Drew, Somerset in the 1940's. Major F. A. Menzies, a surveyor and distinguished British army engineer described what he saw in his journal:

"Although the weather was dull there was no sign of a storm. Just at a moment when I was re-checking a bearing on one of the stones in that group, it was as if a powerful flash of lightning hit the stone, so the whole group was flood-lit, making them glow like molten gold in a furnace. Rooted to the spot – unable to move – I became profoundly awestruck, as dazzling radiations from above, caused the whole group of stones to pulsate with energy in a way that was terrifying. Before my eyes, it seemed the stones were enveloped in a moving pillar of fire – radiating light without heat – writhing upwards towards the heavens: on the other hand it was descending in a vivid spiral effect of various shades of colour – earthward. In fact the moving, flaring lights gyrating around the stones had joined the heavens with the earth."

I really felt that what had happened to Major Menzies was no accident. It was just too powerful a phenomena not to have been made use of.

I realised I didn't really know anything about lightning so, I watched several documentaries and one of them, the National Geographic Lightning documentary, contained some new information which I didn't find anywhere else. Even though it took me off the trail a bit, it not only led me to something beautiful it also gave me a really useful clue.

Scientists know that static electricity builds up in a Cumulonimbus cloud because of the fast movement of warm air particles rising quickly to the great heights of the anvil head (a kind of cloud you can often see coming a mile off), cooling there and then dropping suddenly and rubbing against other particles moving upwards creating huge amounts of static electricity. But, air is not a good conductor of electricity so they can't understand how lightning can cross hundreds of kilometres of air.

Professor Joe Dwyer from the Florida Institute of Technology explained that lightning is just like rubbing your feet on a carpet and then touching a metal door knob with your finger but lightning differs in that "You have to ask yourself: 'where is the finger that's concentrating the charge to produce this spark?' We're having a really hard time figuring out what that finger is."

Because lightning is too elusive to study in depth, Dwyer simulated a series of lightning bolts by shooting a rocket trailing a length of copper wire into a storm cloud. Very quickly a lightning bolt shot down from the cloud like a trail of fire.

When he studied the data he found that each time one of his lightning bolts hit the earth there was a massive surge in X-rays which nobody had noticed before. This led him to look at "cosmic rays", the microscopically-charged particles that are shot across the galaxy from stars which have exploded a million years ago. These rays, millions of which hit the Earth every day, can't be seen or heard but they can be measured because of the X rays they produce as they alter the air's atomic structure allowing them to pass through. From the documentary:

"When a cosmic ray hits a cloud it causes a huge momentary surge in electricity, enough to create a spark. The cosmic ray then hurtles on towards the ground. Superfast moving particles collide with air molecules and rip them apart. For a fraction of a second the air becomes

electrically conductive and provides a path down which the current can run. Now lightning can strike."

In other words, as Joe Dwyer explains, *"If these ideas are correct then there maybe a connection between the lightning that we see and a star exploding half way across the galaxy a million years ago."*

*

Something else I found out is that at it's peak, the temperature of a lightning bolt hits 50,000 degrees and so it literally burns the air. In the heat, nitrogen and oxygen react together to create nitrates, these rain to Earth and provide nutrients for plants. An Aboriginal ranger, in another film I watched about lightning, says that lightning fires are good because they clear the ground and edible wild foods come back.

Such a beautiful thought that cosmic rays from exploding stars half way across the galaxy a million years ago could be the "finger" in the cloud, not only scorching the air and the land with the fires they produce but also enabling new life to come into it.

*

At this point I was beginning to wander off track so I was really glad that my friend Anne Wright came over to have a cup of tea and I excitedly told her the outline of my ideas. "I think the people who designed the stone circles were using the natural phenomena of lightning hitting granite as a kind of demonstration of power. What actually happens during lightning strikes – the halo, the strange fire - sounds far too Biblical not to be made use of. I know that some of the stone circles had lunar and solar alignments so then setting them alight with lightning, like a crown of unearthly fire, must have been the icing on the cake. You could get anyone to do anything for you with a display like that! One idea I had was that maybe the stones were meant to be hit by lightning and toppled over like skittles - it would go with men's love of blowing things up and the bigger the rock toppled, the more powerful you are, sort of thing. Like the largest standing stone at Carnac, the top was taken off by lightning."

Setting the stone circles alight with lightning strikes would make sense of why the stones always look so scruffy, altered as they might be by them, roughened like the amber beads, from so much use.

Then Anne said: "Wouldn't it be difficult to get the lightning to hit the stones?"

I said I didn't think so as I kept coming across incidents of people being hit by lightning near stone circles. I told her that someone a couple of years ago was hit at the Castlerigg stone circle in Keswick and was taken to hospital. When I'd looked for more information about it I'd found a chat room where it was being discussed and a person was saying that she'd sat in the stone circle and watched a sequence of thunderstorms, taking it in turn down the valleys before lashing its forks around them. Everyone had taken cover in their cars whilst she sat alone in the circle. After sometime, one of the forks ruptured next to her and smashed a wall in two 100 yards away. She said it had happen to her at a number sites over the years.

But then I thought about what Anne had said and thought that maybe it *was* a bit slap dash to just hope and pray that the lightning would hit the stones especially if you had gathered a group of people there in order to impress them.

The truly impressive ceremony would be to attract a lightning bolt *at will*.

But who can do that?

Then I remembered that the scientists had actually done this and I thought about how they did it: they'd shot a rocket into a Cumulonimbus cloud, trailing a length of copper wire.

Could Bronze Age man have done anything similar even though he didn't have a rocket?

And then I suddenly realised what he *did* have: Bronze Age man could have shot a bow and arrow trailing a length of copper wire into a storm cloud. It wouldn't have to go far, just as the climbers found on Grand Teton, all you have to do is move a piece of metal in a highly charged atmosphere for it to attract the lightning.

I looked up to see if there is any folklore about men shooting arrows into thunderstorms and found so many iconic images and statues and pages of references that I just looked into the first one listed.

In a book called: The Lineaments of Islam: Studies in Honour of Fred McGraw Donner edited by Paul Cobb it said: *"Shooting arrows into heaven constitutes an ancient ritual; usually the shooters aimed at thunderclouds, or really at the power that dwelled in them and caused lightning to thunder. Herodotus (the "Father of History") writes in Histories Book 4 that Thracians will, during a thunderstorm, shoot arrows at the sky muttering threats against the Lord of Lightning and Thunder because they recognize no God but their own."*

So, there *is* a history of men firing arrows into thunderstorms for religious purposes. A hunter-gatherer would never waste an arrow like that so it had to be from someone under the influence of a civilization.

I imagined how this would be: a man, standing near the stone circle, a halo around his head, bow pulled back, releasing his arrow into the black sky. And then suddenly, out of the blackness, a fiery lightning bolt shoots down from the heavens amid a massive clap of thunder to engulf the ring of stones in fire, glowing like molten gold in a furnace; like a supernatural crown, like a corona around an eclipse of the sun.

Now the people watching would be flat on their faces with fear, a fear that can get the poor sods to dedicate their precious lives to doing utterly pointless things like dragging great stones about the countryside, or looking for black rocks in the mud, all to enhance the power still further of the men who have blinded them with science.

CHAPTER 4

I went up onto the moor and looked at it with this history in mind. If it had been felled and shot about by lightning for over a thousand years that must have been a pretty violent time. The oak and hazel that once grew here have never returned.

I wonder what this sense of power did to men? And their relationship with women? Perhaps men drawing down lightning bolts as though talking to God was when the idea of male superiority began, especially as there's no feminine equivalent to a lightning bolt. It must have been very difficult for the men to stay grounded. It must have been very difficult for the women to believe they still had any power of their own.

There is another kind of stone feature from the Bronze Age which I was keen to try my hand at working out: stone rows. Stone rows are just a series of standing stones set along a line.

If stone circles were celestial crowns then what are stone rows?

Stone rows were erected in the latter part of the Bronze Age and the largest concentration of them is in Carnac, France. There are some on Dartmoor too. They are apparently not aligned to any solar or lunar phases and their purpose is thought to be ceremonial or religious but of course nobody really knows.

At first I'd thought maybe they were linked together with copper wire (easy enough for Bronze Age people to make, especially after they'd added tin which makes copper stronger when it is thin) and so direct the lightning towards a burial mound (which are often at the end of the row) as a way of raising the dead. But that wouldn't last long as an idea because the dead aren't raised; you need something that actually works in order for people to believe in the stories you tell them about who's behind it and what they must do because of it.

I came across an interesting idea in "The Atheists Bible" by Joan Connor that the positively charged spikes rising upwards under a storm cloud that attract the negatively charged ones coming down (which, if they connect, make lightning), were thought of as where the spirits of the dead are believed to traverse. So, "end stones" were put at the entrances to burial sites to block the passage of the spirits and keep them in their boxes (or go into the underworld as per Egyptian culture?). A very interesting story because it made reference to lightning phenomena in their culture. But, it still didn't help me with the stone rows.

If stone circles seemed a bit rough and ready to me (hardly surprising considering what they'd been through) stone rows were positively ugly. They look institutional and cold.

All I knew about them was that the highest number of stone rows is in Carnac, so, what's so special about Carnac? It has the same granite rock as Dartmoor but, unlike Dartmoor, in Carnac nearly all the stones stand near the sea. So, perhaps those who brought the knowledge could have been sea faring people.

In the book "Sea of Knowledge, Stone of Plenty" by John Burke, I found a description of the area which triggered my interest: *"The western part of France is mainly rocks. Geologically, it is part of the Armorican Massif. Rich in granite, quartz and schist it is also loaded with magnetite."*

Magnetite? Where had I come across that word before? Shuffling through reams of papers and notebooks, I finally located it. *Lodestones* are made from magnetite. What's a lodestone? It's the old word for a magnet.

And following my hunch that stone rows would also have something to do with lightning, I looked up "magnets and lightning" and I came up with something very interesting indeed:

Dr Peter Wasilewski, a retired NASA scientist says that lodestones are composed of magnetite which has been struck by lightning.

And what happens when lightning strikes a granite standing stone? Everything around it becomes *magnetic*.

No wonder scientists have established that a magnetic field emanates from the vicinities of megalithic sites if they were deliberately and repeatedly being struck by lightning.

I looked up the earliest known descriptions of magnets and found an explanation in the book "Ancient Inventions" by Peter James and Nick Thorpe that the original discovery of magnetism is ascribed to Thales of Miletus. Him again! This time a story of how it was actually noticed by someone else was with it so it's quite likely that he didn't *discover* amber's properties either. A shepherd boy tending his flocks on the mountain slopes of Magnesia suddenly found he could not move because the nails in his sandals and his metal tipped staff were held fast by magnetic forces in the ground.

Apparently Thales took the trouble to experiment with this force and he found that magnetite attracted iron but only when it had been struck by lightning. He noted the similarity between this action and the fact that, when rubbed, amber attracted feathers and other light objects.

The next thing I asked was did *Egypt* have any need of magnets?

I looked up "Egypt and magnetism" and found, in the book "Secret History of Ancient Egypt", the author Herbie Brennan, says:

"According to the Roman writer Claudian the most spectacular use of magnetism appeared in Egyptian temples.

During the Roman occupation it was found that a temple at Alexandria housed statues of Mars and Venus made from iron and lodestone respectively. Their ceremonial use was magnificent. While music played, Venus was laid reclining on a bed of roses then Mars was slowly brought towards her.

As the magnetic field interacted with the metal, the two deities suddenly sprang together in a passionate embrace.

Still earlier, Pharaoh Ptolemy II commissioned the Greek architect Timochares to create a metallic statue of his Queen that would float in the air, suspended by magnets located in the ceiling and walls of his chamber."

And then I read in the book "Ancient Inventions" that *"There was an image of The Sun God also called Amun, which was floated in the Temple of Serapis in Alexandria, using magnets."*

Thunderbolt city! I nearly fell of my chair again.

So, the Egyptians were creating a magical display of the Sun God by using magnets; by using magnetite that had been made magnetic by being struck by *lightning*.

To keep this display going the Egyptians would need a *supply* of magnets. How often do you come across magnetite that has been struck by lightning when you're just out for a walk? Very rarely, if ever. So, what do you do if you need some?

Somewhere along the line I came across a reference to the fact that there is a town in Egypt called Carnac only it's spelt with a K, just like the Breton spelling of Carnac.

So, I wondered if this Temple of Serapis with the floating image of the Sun God by using magnets, was anywhere near the town in Egypt called Karnac? I looked it up and sure enough in all the vastness of the whole of Egypt, the temple with its floating image is less than a mile away.

I looked up information about this Egyptian Karnac and found that it is the second largest religious site in all the world, with the Sun God "Amun" at its head.

In the Egyptian language, Karnac means "most select of places."

Could Carnac in France be connected with the Karnac in Egypt? Does Carnac fit with the description of being "most select of places"? Well, it is rich in magnetite, it is in a lighting belt and it is right by the sea. I would think it would be a perfect place to get your magnets from.

If you stood a granite rock in the ground, waited for the appearance of an Anvil head on a cloud and then, when your hair stands on end shoot an arrow trailing a copper wire into the air which you've also attached to the standing stone, lighting could come down the wire and hit that stone. If you had surrounded the stone before hand with lots of pieces of magnetite that you've found in the area, those pieces would now become magnetised. And thereafter be called "lodestones".

If you wanted even more lodestones than one standing stone could produce, you would put up more standing stones. If you put them all in a row and you ran copper wire between them then spread the whole area with pieces of magnetite, when any of the standing stones in the row was struck by lightning the whole lot would become magnetised. And you would have a huge number of magnets.

The boat from Egypt would arrive close by and the magnetised rocks are put on board.

I therefore think that the stone rows at Carnac were put up as a magnet factory for the Temple of Serapis in Karnac, Egypt, to ensure that the image of the Sun God "Amun" could continue to float across its ceiling.

It must have created an awesome display of magic in the Temple of Serapis, *so* awesome that even if your belief had begun to wane by the end of a hard week, all you had to do was go to the temple on Sunday and look up at the image of the Sun God floating across the heavens without anyone even touching it, and your faith in magic would be restored.

And so the workers were inspired to work harder.

CHAPTER 5

Perhaps being motivated to work by the use of magic is preferable to the behaviour of today's government who seem to think that pushing people into debt will get them working harder (see Channel 4 News Mhairie Black MP: "Forcing people into hunger does not incentivise work").

But no matter where we are in history, I think there are always two kinds of manipulation at work on us. One is the kind that's thought of by people either in the past or in the present day. For example there is manipulation in every advert, in every campaign, in every label like "free range" or "ethically sourced" or "fat free" or "bargain".

And then there's the kind of manipulation which happens when we are in Nature.

When I take people to a Beech tree and they find out it has an edible nut, they immediately start looking on the ground under the tree to try and find one. They are so completely absorbed in their task that they have forgotten all about their troubles and they are only thinking about finding a Beechnut. All of them do it, I've never seen a person who doesn't do it. I've never seen a person who even tries to resist it or who is sceptical, they just instantly believe the Beechnuts are there somewhere and they will continue looking even when I'm trying to call them on. They don't want to let go. They are caught in the enchanting, magical embrace of the Beech tree and they just want to stay there looking for its treasure.

It's the same with looking for mushrooms or looking for seaweed or mussels or wild strawberries; gathering wild food is like going from one magical embrace to another.

Why would that be? Why would Nature make such powerful embraces?

As far as the Beech tree is concerned, think about what it needs to happen with its seeds that it can't do itself: the seeds are so heavy they fall right beside the tree which is not a good place for a new Beech tree to grow. So, it needs the seeds to be picked up and taken further away.

Making them edible has proven to be a very good way of doing this because what happens, whether you're a squirrel or a human, is that if you find lots of them you will put them in your pocket or in your mouth pouch and eat them somewhere else.

If you've ever tried to peel a Beechnut you'll find that for every ten that get eaten, at least one of them slips out of your grip and gets lost on the ground. And by the law of averages if a tree produces thousands of seeds in an autumn, and has dozens of visitors, at least one of the seeds is going to land in the right place.

This kind of manipulation is based on goodness. The tree might be taking over our mind without us realising it as it keeps us scamping about under its branches looking for treasure but at least what it gives us is very good for us: not only is the nut fun to find, it's oily flavour is delicious to eat giving us moments of heavenly bliss right now as well as good fats for the winter.

And it gives us relief from anguish. Because that's what people have forgotten when they are under the tree looking for nuts; they haven't forgotten their name or their loved ones, they have forgotten their worries. Under a Beech tree it feels like everything will be alright and it feels like we will be taken care of. These are feelings we may not have had since we were children. And when I ask people afterwards what it was like to hunt about for Beechnuts, they always say the same thing: that it made them feel so free, like being a child again and they felt so happy.

What's so ironic is that we are never happier or feel more free than when we are being manipulated by plants. When we do the jobs in Nature that Nature needs us to do it rewards us with pleasure. Gathering wild food isn't about survival at all, it's about *freedom*.

Some people say that if we were all gathering wild food tomorrow there would be none left. But that's not true at all because without people or animals to distribute the seeds there would far fewer naturally occurring wild plants in the world.

When wild *leaves* are edible the job that the plant needs the human or animal to do is to *prune* it by picking its leaves. Then the leaves grow back twice as thickly, just as plants do in the garden, which makes the plant stronger. But somehow people have a mental block about this which means they cannot believe that plants in the wild grow back more thickly after being grazed. So I suggest they pick a stinging nettle top and come back in two weeks time to see what has happened to the stump of the stem. It will have grown back with two heads instead of one so now it's twice as thick with leaves. It's the same with all the edible wild leaves of spring: the more you pick, the more they grow back.

When I explain this on my wild food walks I then ask the group why they think some plants have evolved an edible *root* which means that when you dig it up you are destroying the plant? How is that *helping* the plant? Sometimes a whole group just can't get the answer, other times just one person will ask "Is it so that there'd be more room for the others to grow?" Yes! If you look at all the plants that have edible roots for humans or animals, for example, Burdock or Wild Carrot, they all drop their seeds right beside themselves and so they get clogged up and need thinning out. So, having an edible root means they get thinned out which means their roots are bigger, they then have bigger flower heads and so lots more seeds than if they were thin and spindly.

So when people tell me that if we were all eating wild food tomorrow there would be none left I explain that in reality if we were all eating wild food there would be *twice* as much. We are just tools for Nature and when we do the jobs we've evolved to do we feel completely happy and completely free and there will always be wild food for tomorrow.

*

I went for a swim through the woods in a long still stretch of the river and I noticed the surface of the water around me was covered in seeds. I was thinking about how they'd got there and realised they were blown there by the wind. So they were *sown* by the wind. And if they were sown by the wind what about all the other jobs that are needed in order to grow plants? How are they done in Nature? The digging and fertilising is done by animals, the watering is done by rain, the sowing is done by the wind, the growing is done by the sun and the moon, the harvesting is done by the animals and so on.

It's just like a giant farm but it isn't creating money. So if the world is just one giant farm but nobody is earning a living from it what's the point of it all? What's the point in going to all that trouble of life starting around the warm vents in the ocean, evolving into all manner of sea creatures that eventually eat the seaweed and come out of the sea and eat the land plants and other animals, and mate, raise young and die and on and on and on? What is the point? What is the point of life and what is the point of the planet?

So I asked myself why do *I* do anything? And I realised that there are only ever two reasons why I do anything: either I *have* to do something or I *want* to do it. If I have to do it I don't tend to put all my energy into it, I just put in enough to get the job done so that I can get on with something that I do want to do. If I do want to do something I usually put everything into it. Why do I do that? Because it feels good.

When I look at everything in Nature doing their jobs, they all look like they're feeling good too: the seeds looked very happy, even on the water; the leaves look very happy on the trees beaming with bright green light; the birds look very happy flying from one branch to another; the clouds look very happy turning from one form to another. And when things are happy they are creating something: they are creating *love*.

If the planet was one giant farm creating love, what would be the effect?

So then I asked myself what is the effect of love on *me*? When I am feeling love I feel like I can do anything, I feel like I am completely capable and I always will be, I feel expanded inside and opened by it. As I'm being opened by love more love comes out and it beats out into the world and joins with all the love that's out there and I feel totally connected to it and it feels like it enters back into me.

To me, love feels *expansive*.

If love is doing this for me it's probably doing this for everything else too. And if every part of Nature is creating *love*, that must amount to a lot of expansive energy being generated every moment of every day and sometimes well into the night.

We know that the universe is expanding but nobody knows what's causing it. What if the love that's being generated by life on the planet is actually expanding the universe? Wouldn't that make perfect sense? Wouldn't that make sense of life and the reason for the planet? That it expands the universe so there's more of it? Just like eating wild food makes more of it too.

I was sharing this thought with my friend Mary Maguire and she said "That's exactly what all the major religions are saying – that love is the creative force behind the universe." But, as so often happens with religion, it's *based* on something that's real but it gets slightly altered for the benefit of those who are using it to manipulate others and so it doesn't really make sense and so you are required to take huge leaps of faith in order to believe it.

I think the reality is that every living thing is creating the universe, by generating love as a by product of doing what makes them happy.

And I think that every living thing can create love, no matter how dire the circumstances, if they know the three questions to ask themselves which will always lead them to it.

Just as the *separation* from Nature (which I wrote about in "The Hunter-Gatherer Way") had three parts to it, so I think the *creation* of Nature has three parts to it too. These parts come in the form of three questions. I think these questions are what every wild thing on the planet asks itself every moment of its life and which get it what it wants most and, as a result, it generates love and expands the universe.

We can ask these questions too but, they are not always easy for everyone to *answer* because of our separation from our own nature which has been done by conditioning.

So, the three questions that lead to love go like this: first of all you must ask yourself: what am I *actually* experiencing?

This is more tricky than it sounds because a lot of the time we have been conditioned to believe what we are *told* we will experience which is often nothing like the reality at all. For example: when Elsa was little I invited one of her school friends for a walk with us up on the moor. As soon as the little girl got out of the car she started screaming about all the mud. It had been such a dry autumn that the path was made of hard packed earth. But the little girl was in such a state of despair that I asked her "*Where* is the mud? Point to the mud."

She started looking all around her but she couldn't see any mud. When she realised this she stopped crying, relaxed and came along happily. I later found out that her mother was a city-type person who has a white carpet on her sitting room floor. She had never been up on the moor because she believed it was covered with mud which would spoil her carpet and she had instilled this so strongly in the mind of her child that even when her child was experiencing something *completely different*, she saw only what she *imagined* was there.

Our imagination has been programmed by all sorts of people during the last 4,000 years; stuffed full of fears and nonsense by whoever wanted us to do a job for them. But unless you are able to see through this conditioning and recognise what you are *actually* experiencing you won't be able to do anything about it.

So, how can you see through the conditioning? You can help to by-pass whatever conditioning has been put in there by deliberately activating your senses. By activating more of your senses than just your eyesight you are more likely to recognise the reality because you've got more information to go on than just your imagination.

So, how do you activate your senses?

This is much easier to do in the outdoors because there's more to stimulate all the senses than indoors. All you have to do is just go outside and close your eyes. As soon as you shut off your eyesight, all your other senses immediately get turned up. Suddenly you will be able to *hear*. There will be all kinds of wildlife that were there when you had your eyes open but you just couldn't hear them. You will also be able to tell what the weather is going to do because your skin sensors suddenly get turned up so you can *feel* the wind and the way it is caressing your skin which tells you what it is about to do.

If you then open your eyes and go for a walk without speaking, your mind isn't relying on it's programming but on the sensations you are *actually* experiencing.

So then you can ask yourself the next question which is: how *good* is it?

This is not a question we are encouraged to ask because a lot of us have been programmed to just put up with discomfort. It's almost sacrilege to think we might be worthy of comfort. But ask it and you will get a clear picture of how good the experience is or, in many cases, how not good it is.

So then you can ask yourself the third question which is: from here how will I find *heavenly bliss?*

I believe that asking these three questions will lead to love no matter how dire the circumstances. For example, there were some Polar Bears I read about in the news. With the ice flows melting and nothing left to eat, the Polar bears came onto land looking for food. There they met some Brown bears who showed them which things are good to eat. And now they have started to mate.

Whilst newscasters will speak of this using terms like: "Polar Bears forced onto land" yes, they were but perhaps the bears got themselves to land because they were thinking like this: "What am I *actually* experiencing? There is no more ice. How good is it? Not good at all. How will I find heavenly bliss? Get myself to land and hope for the best." They made their way to land and sure enough, in the arms of the friendly Brown bears they found there, they found food and hugs. And love was the result.

This is the hunter-gatherer way.

I think these three questions are not only what every living wild thing is asking itself throughout it's day as it's guide to getting what it needs but that it's always been this way in Nature. I think these three questions are what have *driven* evolution. And they will continue to drive it, on passed the appalling destruction we are wrecking on the planet.

Perhaps we are wrecking the planet because we are trying to find these questions but they have been buried under 4,000 years of nonsense.

If we ask them of ourselves now and if we trust our instincts that heavenly bliss lies somewhere for us in Nature, we will find that Nature rewards us with a magic that enchants us every day. There will be treasure hunts and delicious flavours and feelings of pure happiness and freedom. And they exist under every Beech tree or within every hedge or along the edge of every sea.

When we are being manipulated by plants to prune them or thin them out or distribute their seeds we are not only ensuring there will be more wild food for tomorrow we are also able to lay down the burdens we carry for a while. Without that awful weight on our backs, we are free to gather wild food. And the more wild food we eat the more goodness we will have in our bellies, and the stronger will be the fire in our hearts, the brighter the diamonds that dance in our eyes and the more love we will create in the world. *Stars Shine*

This is the hunter-gatherer way, the *beat* of a different drum.

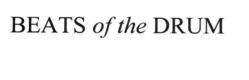

BEATS *of the* DRUM

These are little stories and observations of magical moments written over the last four laps I've made of "The Ring of the Wild Food Year" migration route. I haven't given them dates so that you can hear the change of seasons by the wild foods in them.

I got into the habit of putting the phrase "This is the hunter-gatherer way" at the end of each one because it brought the thought into the context of the bigger picture. Some of them were posted on my blog, "The Hunter-Gatherer Way by Ffyona Campbell" on Facebook.

I've also included some readers reactions to the "Hunter-Gatherer Way" book; some experiences people have shared with me after being taught about wild food on my courses; some reactions from audiences I've given talks to; as well as questions people have asked.

I hope you enjoy them.

We've just feasted on wild food, hunted for and gathered from along the banks of the mighty River Dart.

The group I took with me didn't think we'd find much in this barren winter landscape but they've all gone away completely full now.

Finding wild food all depends on how you look and where you look for it and whether or not you really *believe* it's there.

This is the hunter-gatherer way.

From my wild food market stall, I watched a rather gaunt, shaven headed, tattooed young man tentatively eat his first Primrose.

As sweet pleasure and surprise swept across his face he was completely transformed into a handsome prince.

This is the hunter-gatherer way.

Cakes will comfort for a few mouthfuls but wild food will comfort every part of you for hours and hours and leave you feeling like you've stepped into an everlasting embrace.

This is the hunter-gatherer way.

Wild food is the food of the gods.

This is the hunter-gatherer way.

If you are feeling a bit melancholy this winter, when you go out for a walk, keep your eyes open for a plant that looks just like a stinging nettle but has large white, rounded flower buds on the stem between the leaves.

This is the *Archangel*. If you eat it or drink its juice, it will lift your spirits and "maketh the heart merrie".

It will soon have you smiling again (inside and out).

Just pick a couple (even though they look like stinging nettles they don't sting), put them in a teapot, pour on boiling water, let sit for a few minutes then drink it and wait....

This is the hunter-gatherer way.

If you haven't got any energy and the thought of a whole new year swinging into action fills you with dread, just eat the early edible wild leaves and flowers and they will give you the punch, the laughter and the clarity of thought that all the wild animals are getting right now - that's what all the singing's about.

This is the hunter-gatherer way.

We had a top chef on the wild food walk today. His verdict on the soup we made from our barren landscape gatherings was: *"Delicious!"* He's even going to put it on the menu.

Did you know that the top restaurant in the world is a *wild food* restaurant?

Wild food is the most heavenly food on Earth.

This is the hunter-gatherer way.

Have you ever wondered what the birds are singing about in the dawn chorus?

Have you ever been amazed at the sheer output from those little tiny bodies?

They must have amazing lungs to be able to sing like that. *Amazing* lungs.

What do they use their lungs for? To fly of course. When you fly and you get tired you can't just sit down and have a rest, you have to be able to keep going especially if you are small and the wind catches you.

I think the birds are singing at dawn to warm up their lungs ready for the day.

And their songs are all different because they all fly in a different way, so in a way each of them is saying "This is the song of my flight!"

This is the hunter-gatherer way.

Amazing that "The Hunter-Gatherer Way" is appealing to men and women equally: the bushcrafters and the hedgewitches, side by side.

This is the hunter-gatherer way.

For 6 weeks last summer, I stopped eating wheat, dairy and sugar because I wanted to feel the full effect of eating seaweed and I suspected that these modern foods would interfere with it.

As the days went by I felt myself becoming much clearer in thought, and in movement, and after every wild food meal I experienced growing sensations of bliss. It was heaven.

But, one week-end life got in the way and I ate several ice-creams on the beach. Not only did I get the expected stomach cramps and sense of depression, but I also got massively sunburnt. I had been as brown as a berry all summer but now my skin was red and sore and stinging.

What had happened?

We know that what makes us brown is a hormone, melanin. It would make sense then that if we are eating a *hormonal food* – like milk - then the hormones we need to produce to tan could very well be interfered with.

So I think its quite likely that we get sunburnt in our own climate because we eat dairy products, and eating ice-cream on the beach must be the worst.

Being aware of the hormones we put into our blood will not only save us from the hell of hormonal imbalance but will also lead us to the long forgotten heavens of our lives.

This is the hunter-gatherer way.

Imagine eating a salad that raises your metabolism, lowers your cholesterol, tastes like heaven on earth and sets your mind free. I bet you've never seen that description on a bag from the supermarket.

This is *wild* food. And it's free.

Free from being forced; free from being restricted; free from EU regulations; free from being nipped in the bud whenever it wants to shoot into flower and spread its seeds on the wind...and in being so free, it is the very *best* it can ever be.

You are what you eat and when you eat wild food it allows your mind to escape, to break free from under the plastic.

This is the hunter-gatherer way.

Have you ever wondered why you suit some colours and not others?

The answer became clear to me when, for my birthday, I had my colours 'done' by a colour practitioner who held up different coloured scarves to my face to see which ones suited me.

I suddenly realised that all the colours I suited were of the colours of the western isles of Scotland – the soft, dusky colours of a landscape in the mist, the heathers, the peaty earth, the hazy sea.

My father's family is from there and I have his colouring.

It would make sense from a hunter-gatherer point of view because suiting the colours of my homeland means I would blend in with them and not stand out. In other words, I would be *camouflaged.*

And so when I look in the mirror, I see the colours that have kept my family alive, able to hunt and to avoid being hunted.

While wearing clothes of my colours I don't even see my arms swinging as I walk, I feel like I have melted into Nature and everything around me seems to relax and accept me into it.

This is the hunter-gatherer way.

Yesterday I was drinking from a fast flowing stream in a deeply shaded, green leafy glade, surrounded by bluebells, on Dartmoor. (I don't suggest anyone else does this because of the threat of liver fluke.)

As I drank I realised the water tasted of the perfume of wild flowers. How could this be? Then I realised it was because of the pollen, floating on the wind and landing in the stream, all along its course.

And I thought of the many friends I have who have sworn by the natural anti-histamines in nettle flowers to help them with hay fever.

And I thought of homeopathy, that seemingly bizarre idea of diluting natural substances in large quantities of water to make them stronger......

And so I wondered, could it be that our streams are actually running with the homeopathic antidotes to the seasons?

This is the hunter-gatherer way.

I love watching the head of a dribble of water as it negotiates its way down a rough surface: how when it gets stuck it waits until all the water behind it gets down to swell it into a larger mass of strength so it can go over the top; or how if it can't get over, it rolls itself sideways till it reaches a place to flow on down; and how, when it goes, it runs so fast, so freely, so joyfully.

How utterly confident it is, there isn't a shred of self-doubt.

How clear its goal is, how strong its will.

How, at every obstacle, it's working things out just like us.

This is the hunter-gatherer way.

For many winters now, I've looked after a small farm on Dartmoor and I noticed how the dogs would behave differently on the nights when it rained: they would sleep. Deeply. Not even an ear open, sprawled out heavily across the dog-bed, snoring.

On all the other nights they'd wake me countless times when they heard something outside and they'd bark suddenly, throw themselves at the door and race outside into the dark to chase after it.

How did they know that when it rains there's nothing to worry about?

Because, I realised, the things they are chasing don't like getting their feet wet. You can see this on the little trails through the woods, all the animals use the same path: the badgers, the foxes, the rabbits, the pheasants, and when they get to a wet bit, they all walk around it.

So now when it rains at night, I think of all the creatures curled up in their warm, dry, earthy burrows having a night off, just like the dogs.

This is the hunter-gatherer way.

Have you ever noticed that when it rains there are no shadows?
This is the hunter-gatherer way.

Last year I was learning about the Apogee and Perigee of the Moon - how it travels on an egg-shaped path around the Earth so that sometimes its far Away (Apogee) and at other times it's close too.

As I was learning, the Moon was at the Perigee and at the time it was full. I noticed we were suddenly having some unusually stormy, rainy and windy weather then, after a lovely long warm spell.

I happened to be talking to a yachtsman and so I asked him if the Moon affects the weather. He said it doesn't and explained to me, over and over again how the *Sun* affects the weather.

I thought he was missing the point so I looked it up on line and found a book on it called "The Lunar Code" by Ken Ring. I bought it, devoured it and gave it to the yachtsman. He hasn't given me his response to it yet.

Ken Ring, a New Zealander, noticed that there *is* indeed a direct correlation between the Moon and the weather and after a huge amount of work, he realised what it is...the Moon doesn't just affect the ocean's tides it also affects the *atmospheric tides*.

The Syndey to Hobbart yacht race was wiped out by massive storms one year. Ring noticed that it was held on a Perigee full Moon. The next year the race was also run on the Perigee full Moon and again there were massive storms and many lives were lost. He contacted the race organisers and pointed this out to them and now, apparently, they consult him first.

According to Ring's research, every major flood in recorded history has happened at the time of the Perigee full Moon.

This is the hunter-gatherer way.

If you think about it, the Royal family live more like hunter-gatherers than anyone else: they hunt and shoot and fish; they eat the finest foods on Earth like lobster and caviar and wild salmon; they change residence every season; they surround themselves with vast areas of unspoilt countryside; their things are handmade out of 100% natural materials and they don't carry any money.

This is the hunter-gatherer way.

I went looking for Corner Berries this morning - just walked out the door and along the lane, no basket, no bag, just me and the sunshine. I love going out like this because everything seems to be much more delighted with me, and I with it.

And I love making sudden "Oooh!" sounds as the red berries pop into view and "Mmm!" sounds if I discover that one of them has the gentle, sweet mellowness I always wait with great anticipation for as I let the berry slowly dissolve a little on my tongue, before fully relaxing and deeply enjoying the rest of it.

And then, after many hours, to wander home, empty handed and full bellied.

Happy days.

And if you are wondering what a Corner Berry is, some people call them Wild Strawberries but I think that is a useless name as you don't find them in straw in the wild, but you do find an awful lot of them on corners.

This is the hunter-gatherer way.

Something very special happened on a Seaweed Wild Food Walk yesterday.

It happened after we'd looked at all the seaweed and had gone inland from the sea, barefoot over the hot rocks to the beach to look for the ancestors of our garden vegetables – the Wild Carrots, Wild Spinach, Fat Hen etc.

But unknown to us the sand had become so hot it was almost melting. By the time we realised how hot it was we were too far away from any relief: there was no shade and no sea - it being low tide and a long way out over the searing hot rocks.

I quickly went ahead, gathered the plants I wanted to show them and quickly returned. I hoped they would be OK, I hoped they would somehow manage to cope with their bare feet on such hot sand perhaps by doing a jig.

But when I returned, I found them quite happy, standing around chatting calmly and when I looked down I saw their feet were ankle deep in the sand; the soles of their feet in the cool wetness deep underneath.

It made me realise that a very important thought process had gone on for them: the torture must have become so unbearable they were forced to look for a solution.

They hadn't panicked because they had *instinctively* known there must be relief somewhere, if only they could work out where it was.

They must have scouted around in their minds with lightning speed, and suddenly realised the solution was right under their feet.

A wonderful ah-ha! moment must have followed when they realised they'd found *heavenly bliss* just inches below what had become a burning hell.

And for their belief and their clever thinking, Nature had rewarded them ten fold.

On the way back up the hill, they all walked so tall.

This is the hunter-gatherer way.

Someone recently told me how much he had loved the dedication in my third book, "The Whole Story" and it made me really happy to think about it again because I had come off the path lately and was feeling pretty lost and despondent.

I had dedicated it to "The spirits of my ancestors who watch over me and who come in many forms."

I wrote that dedication 15 years ago and I realised that as time has gone on, I've actually added a whole new layer of understanding to this. The discovery of it came to me while I was working-out in the gym. I was taking two very different kinds of classes: one was a yoga-type class and the other a kick boxing class (with Karen Ouzie the world champion, no less!). Because Karen is *so* powerful, the class was extremely hard with many muscle burning sections.

Completely fed up with the mental anguish I always had to go through during the "arms in the air for 10 minutes section", I decided to try something I'd noticed in the yoga-class: to just *relax* during the burn and let the blood move into the place that I'm working.

And it worked! Not only was I completely released from the mental and physical hell of having my arms up in the air for so long, I was actually thriving there! I had found the way to cross-over from hell into *heavenly bliss*.

And the more I loved it, the more I felt that a whole army of my ancestors were with me, delighted with me, making me smile with pride, and pirouette inside, and willing me on. And they always came in their most magnificence whenever my blood was up and working its hardest.

What is our blood anyway but the makings of all of our family before us? It contains the parts of them that are still alive. We add to it too and pass it on to our children who then become its keepers and that's what we're actually doing on Earth – being vessels for keeping our family blood alive.

And when that blood is worked we are activating it, releasing its power and energy and life, we are using whatever has been left in our blood by all those who have gone before us.

So that when you burn you are feeling your ancestors awakening.

Ironic really that to call on the Spirits of our Ancestors all we have to, in the burning fires of hell on Earth, is simply relax.

This is the hunter-gatherer way.

An interesting question from a reader who is just waiting for a copy of "The Hunter-Gatherer Way" book:

"I've read a lot recently the works of many anthropologists and archaeologists who estimate that an 80/20 split exists i.e. that 80% of food retrieval is gathering and done by women and 20% is hunting, which is overwhelmingly done by men.

Hunting is viewed as unreliable/unpredictable - could be an analogy for the male of the species - and so I now use the phrase Gatherer/Hunters to reflect this ratio of importance to the survival of the species and to acknowledge that it is women who are contributing 4x as much to that survival, at the very least in respect of food - including water, which is pretty fundamental I think its fair to say. I just wondered if you have any thoughts on this?" *Mick Mack*

My response was:

Hi Mick,

My view of this is that men and women have very different kinds of energy: women like to work steadily, in rhythm while pounding and kneading and washing and in the company of other women, and can keep this up all day long, chatting and singing to turn the drudgery into fun.

This kind of energy brings to the table the greens, grains, nuts, fruits, roots, seaweeds, lichens etc and anything that needs to be processed.

Men, on the other hand, like to use a huge amount of energy all in one go and then collapse. This kind of energy is perfect for hunting and it contributes the meat. So, each of the sexes provides a different kind of food which together is a balanced meal.

In the hunter-gatherer societies I have encountered, no one sex is favoured above another. They are equal; equally valued and equally respected. I imagine that if a man got cocky with his hunting prowess, the women could easily put him back in line as they are the ones who know the poisons.

I really look forward to your thoughts about it when you've read the book.

Ffyona Campbell

Unlike in the Western world where we cover our footpaths with small stones, there are virtually no small stones on the footpaths of Africa.

Almost everyone is barefoot (the people and the animals) and so if you see a stone, you pick it up and throw it away. It makes the footpaths feel like velvet.

This is the hunter-gatherer way.

Watching the mighty electrical muscles of lightning bolts stretch out and ripple across the night sky makes me even more upset at how we have captured yet another magnificent force in Nature and enslaved it to work for us - imagine this magnificence being channelled into having to mow the lawn, or heat up an iron or a buzz an electric toothbrush.

But worse than that, harnessing electricity has robbed us of our need for the energy of *young* people. It used to be that young people were the powerhouses of our community - their energy was *phenomenal* and as we grew older we relied on them to do the work we could no longer do, just as they relied on us to tell them what needed to be done and how to do it. They knew they were needed and that they had a part to play and they *loved* it.

But then we replaced our need of them with electricity and less than 100 years on look at them now - many of them walk around with their trousers hanging down, some having to take drugs just to feel loved and wanted, some having to self-harm to numb the emotional pain.

Why is *anyone* trying to find yet more ways to generate electricity?

The *only* truly renewable form of energy is our own physical energy because the more we use of it, the more we have.

This is the hunter-gatherer way.

How someone's fear led to a wonderful experience: as we headed out on a seaweed wild food walk this week, I noticed that one of the women had quickly fallen behind. I wondered if she was having problems with walking barefoot, so I waited for her.

But, as it turned out, she was engaged with something far worse: she was fighting back her fear that there was something lurking in the water under the seaweed around her feet.

Feeling very shaky, she was trying to push through her fears. She had driven hundreds of miles to be here but the experience was turning out to be very unpleasant indeed.

All of us wanted her to succeed and we tried the usual things like reassuring her there wasn't anything to be afraid of but, it wasn't enough, the fear had taken hold. So, I wondered if there was something I'd seen other people do from other ways of life which might help her.

My mind rested on an experience I'd had of balancing a bucket of water on my head. I'd seen women doing this in Africa of course, and they'd looked so graceful and calm that once I was back in the UK and missing Africa very much, I'd tried it out myself.

I found that if I placed a rolled up drying-up cloth on my head first, then the bucket half filled with water and just relaxed, not only was there a rod of strength thrusting its way down through my body to make it perpendicular so that the water would remain horizontal, it also demanded that I *believe* in myself (or else the bucket would just wobble and fall off) and, because I had to hold my head *up* to keep the bucket level, I couldn't actually *see* what I was about to step on.

This abandonment of my bare feet to their fate had instantly brought incredible new sensations of warmth and softness from their sensors that I'd never noticed before when I'd been looking down at the ground and anticipating only sharp objects and pain. By taking my eyes off it, another sensory detector had been activated.

So, I suggested to this very brave woman that she balance her gathering basket on the top of her head. Gamely, she agreed.

To keep her company, I did it too and as soon as I couldn't see what I was about to step onto my feet became very different gatherers of information: they automatically slid slowly forward with their soles always in touch with the surface, assessing with consummate ease the security of every possible footstep. The texture of the seaweed felt so deeply succulent, the quality of the warmth so deeply calming that both of us forgot completely about what might be lurking there to nip us on the toe and relaxed instead into this total body experience.

When it came time to head back from the edge of the sea to the shore, I looked back to see how this brave and determined woman was coping with the thought of doing it all again. She was holding back again, but not because she was afraid, but because she loved it so much she didn't want to leave. With the tide coming in gently around her and over her knees now, she seemed completely united with it, melting into it and simply radiating with peace and pleasure.

This is the hunter-gatherer way.

Taking a break between teaching Seaweed Wild Food walks last week, I went up to Dartmoor for a barefoot walk.

After a while, the animal trail I was following led me into a bog. The reeds were so long I couldn't see the best way out so I looked around and noticed a small mound about 4 feet high which I could climb for a good view to work out how to precede.

But, once I got to the foot of the mound, it took me about half an hour to get to the top of it because, after just two footsteps, I realised that the whole thing was absolutely *covered* in Whortleberries.

I had to stop and try one to see if it was ripe. It was: sweet and delicious. I looked around to make sure I was in no danger if I stayed for a while and, as all was well, I settled myself to picking them. Smiling happily I realised how quickly my fortunes had changed from *angst* and *frustration* to *heavenly bliss* in just two easy footsteps.

But, after a while I became aware that I was sitting in the wind, so, realising there was an improvement to be had on even this, the most glorious of hillocks, I made my way round the to lea side - out of the wind. When I got there, not only did the wind cease and the sun warm me sweetly but the butterflies danced like marionettes and the Whortleberries were even *bigger* and even *more* juicy on this side of the hill. *Heavenly bliss!*

I sighed a lot, and smiled a lot, and popped them into my mouth a lot, and after a while I realised that it's not actually possible to completely strip a bush of berries in the wild because there comes a point when you get *bored* with that particular patch and have to move on. What a very useful piece of programming we come into the world with. And I thought about the many years I've spent lashing myself to be disciplined and thoroughly finish something when in fact my natural tendencies to move on to the next thing, might well have an important role to play when Nature takes the world back – getting bored of a patch means there's plenty left for everyone who comes after you, and for you after *them*.

As I continued my journey - a small nip across a stream and out of the bog and up the hill along the animal trail again - I passed a man-made hole about 6 feet deep and 10 feet across. It was probably the remains of a mine of some sort, the treasures it once held now gone.

I peeped over the edge and saw that it too was covered with Wortleberries. Carefully assessing the hole to make sure it was just a hole and not a mine-shaft, I climbed down into it. The heat in there was like another country - warm and dry and still. The whole thing was so full of plump blue Whortleberries that I realised Nature had transformed this ugly scar from Man's insatiable greed and turned it into a giant bowl of wild fruit.

How beautiful and perfect. And the more wild food I ate, the more beautiful and perfect it got.

This is the hunter-gatherer way.

I've just put all four of my books on my website for people to be able to buy them. 30 years of work set neatly in a row. What a journey!

The urgency with which I walked around the world makes perfect sense to me now that I've written "The Hunter-Gatherer Way". I knew I was looking for something and that I couldn't rest until I'd found it.

The all-consuming push *ever-onwards!* has been gently replaced by a deep and certain knowledge that I have found what I was looking for.

A heavy price was paid, I thank *goodness* this book is touching people's souls.

Now that the wild mushroom season has begun, I am reminded of an incident that happened a few years ago when my daughter and I were walking into the woods, each with a stick and a basket.

Coming towards us was a young family. The children were skipping joyfully, their arms were full of kindling; their mother was carrying a basketful of wild mushrooms and their father was walking slightly behind.

After they'd passed us, the father called out to me:

"Excuse me, but I wonder if you could verify our finds for us?"

He didn't know me and I didn't know him but he just assumed that because I had a basket and a stick and a daughter that I knew what I was doing.

I was pleased to help and told him to lay out everything on the ground and we would go through them.

As he did so, the family told me they'd never been mushrooming before but that morning they'd met a man in the woods who'd told them they could gather anything with a brown cap, cook them up and they'd be delicious. The children proudly displayed the kindling sticks with which they were going to light their cooking fire.

I looked at the assembled mess of putrefying fungus and explained that even edible mushrooms become poisonous when they are saturated with water and have begun to rot so, most of them were now poisonous. Amongst the remaining, they had a deadly Panther Cap fungus.

They were shocked. The realisation of what they had been about to do slowly sinking in as I explained the possibly fatal consequences of eating them.

I suggested they go on a course to learn the basics but I had a feeling they wouldn't, they seemed to be saying they couldn't be bothered with courses. They wanted to entrust the lives of their family to a complete stranger they met in the woods just because she had a stick.

This frightening disregard for wild mushrooms is alarming, it has never happened in the history of the world before and must have been brought on by the ease with which celebrity chefs use these special ingredients. Whilst I might be quite relaxed about experimenting with some things, wild mushrooms aren't one of them.

I was very lucky to have started my learning by going out every week-end one autumn with Ray Mears. He taught me so well and I never forgot what I learned because years later, when I picked up the trail again, the knowledge was still there and I've added to it, year after year.

But if you haven't got someone to go with and you can't go on a course, perhaps just finding wild mushrooms as they pop into view is quite magical enough without eating them. There is a sweet secret that even many experienced mushrooms hunters don't know, about how to find them:

Mushrooms are the fruiting body of mycelium - the fine white filaments you can sometimes see in the ground which break-down decaying matter. But when the mycelium reaches an obstacle it can't cross, like a stream or a footpath, it puts up a mushroom to send out spores on the wind to cross the obstacle so it can continue in the ground on the other side.

So, looking along the edges of anything is where you will find wild mushrooms.

It also helps to be barefoot. Barefoot you can feel the subtle variations of moisture and warmth in the ground and you greatly reduce the risk of trampling all over the mushrooms you haven't yet seen. If you get stabbed and scratched by brambles and sharp stones, it simply means you need to *slow* down. The slower you go, the more chance you will have of seeing the mushrooms.

Taking a child with you also helps: children and mushrooms seem to have an affinity with each other and I don't think it's just because children are nearer the ground and can see them more easily, there also seems to be a shared delight in simply being alive. I remember finding a Penny Bun mushroom that had come up with an oak leaf on its head and it just looked so pleased with itself that if I'd been a child I'm sure I would have heard it laughing.

All the children I've taught on my courses have been quick as lightening to spot even the most subtle of differences. Children are designed like this. They are also designed to understand the words: DO NOT EAT ANYTHING UNLESS AN ADULT HAS VERIFIED IT FOR YOU BECAUSE IF YOU DO YOU COULD DIE.

It is a very special relationship when an adult and a child can walk into the woods together and both have some important skill to contribute to having a magical time: the child with his or her ability to find the mushrooms and the adult with his or her experience of how to confirm their identity and uses.

Perhaps this need that one generation will always have for the other is the true magic of the wild mushroom.

This is the hunter-gatherer way.

About 10 years ago, whilst mushrooming intensely along the ground, I happened to look up and see a gleaming spot of golden sunlight on an old oak tree and within it was the most beautiful Chicken of the Woods fungus I've ever seen.

I quickly went home to get a knife.

Hurrying as fast as I could in case someone else had seen it in the meantime (despite having not seen anyone all day), and excitedly thinking through all the ingredients of my favourite recipe and whether I had enough of everything, I got back to find that it had gone. Someone had beaten me to it.

Ever since that sad day, whenever I pass that tree, I always look up at it hoping that one day I'll see another glorious, golden Chicken of the Woods fungus.

And then yesterday, there it was! Gleaming and spectacular, and this time I had a knife.

It was a very large Chicken of the Woods.

In the hours that followed, I tried to justify taking all of it by telling myself that last time nobody had left any for me, and that I'd been watching that tree for 10 years now and so this was surely payment enough to make it mine.

But, a small voice started up in my head with the idea of how sweet it would have been if I had checked my overwhelming urge and at least left half of it on the tree.

It would have been the very best way to leave a message to the person who had taken it the first time and who was no doubt also watching that tree.

He or she would have understood and learned from it and beautiful things would have entered the world as a result; deeds as beautiful as this glorious golden fungus and as worthy of all the sweet pleasure it brings.

This is the hunter-gatherer way.

When Elsa was about 5, she was picking blackberries and learning to put them in her basket rather than eating them all at once.

She had noticed that when you see a *huge* blackberry deep inside the bush, you must stop before you shoot your hand in to get it and check first that a spider hasn't woven his web across the entrance because they always seem to do this in front of the biggest fruit.

And then she made another discovery, one that only a child could make: deeply scratched from the brambles thorns, she intuitively looked for something to relieve the pain. She took a soft, juicy blackberry out of her basket and rubbed it on the hot, dry, stinging scratch. The cooling juice and soft applicator of the berry was the perfect antidote bringing *heavenly bliss* to the fires of hell. Clever girl.

All children are clever until the stupid modern world hammers them flat, squashes any sign of spirit, and drills into them that there is nothing to believe in and no relief from suffering except by making money.

No matter where you are, Nature isn't far away. Brambles have such powerful muscles they can push themselves into the world, even through concrete, coming to rescue the children.

This is the hunter-gatherer way.

Have you noticed any spiders this week?

A small one suddenly appeared on the wall by the light switch, another one has parked itself at eye level by the back door, and apparently there's one the size of a fist under the sofa.

I said "That's it then, the spider season has begun" and looked up at the ceiling. Sure enough there was a small dark thing right in the corner. I looked in all the corners and, with Cowboys and Indians music suddenly paying in my head, I realised we were surrounded.

I think that spiders are just about the scariest things in creation: whenever I see one, it makes me jump. Why do they do that?

I think their appearance is designed to make us jump because a spider is a small thing and we are big things and so they are in danger of being squashed. They can't buzz to let us know they're there, so they scare us instead.

But, why have they suddenly appeared in our houses?

I once asked a group of 9 year old children and none of them could figure it out, not even their teacher. So I showed them how to do it, the hunter-gatherer way: you must always ask a mystery a series of questions. For example you could start by asking:

What do spiders like to eat?

Flies, mostly.

What do flies do at this time of year?

Start flying very slowly around the house, crashing into things.

Why? Because they are coming to the end of their lives and they are trying to crash into something that will kill them.

Walking back from school drop off in the early morning this week, I saw the spider's delicate webs picked out in white dew in the hedgerows. They don't just place them randomly though, some of them use bait and place their webs across the entrance to large, soft, juicy blackberries. Why? Because the large ones are beginning to ferment, attracting tiny flies so the spiders place their nets across the entrance to them in the brambles and catch them trying to get to the fruit. Spiders must have a good nose for decaying fruit.

I watched one working on its repairs and it seemed to be using some of its legs like human fingers, counting the threads. I'm sure it was counting because when you're weaving a pattern, you have to carry sets of numbers in your head and the way it did it somehow reminded me of my mother's expression when she would stop knitting and use her fingers to count the number of stitches.

The spider was working so intensely, and the more I watched it, the more I realised it looked just like a fisherman repairing his net.

Webs are very much like nets.

So, I realised that spiders aren't really sinister, scary, menacing hunters but simply fishermen, casting their nets in the sky.

This is the hunter-gatherer way.

I've just noticed that the backs of my hands have an amazing sheen on them, it's like Mother of Pearl on a suntan. I wonder if its because I've been gathering and eating so much seaweed this summer.

Wild food often changes the colour of my hair too: in spring it has a pink tinge to it and I once noticed the same colour in the hair of someone on one of my spring wild food walks. I asked her if she was already eating wild food and she was, lots of it.

Her name was Karen and she told me that during this summer, having eaten a lot of seaweed too, she'd noticed her hair has a deep orange/gold to it, as has mine.

I remember one wonderful autumn eating nothing but wild mushrooms cooked in garlic and butter and Greek yoghurt. Every day I would head out to hunt for them without having breakfast, the hunger would sharpen my eyesight so that I could be home by late morning with a basketful and cook them up and feast and collapse with heavenly bliss. And then, once I could stand up again, I'd go out hunting for more.

I did this every day for two weeks and every morning, when I looked in the mirror, I saw that my hair was turning more and more chestnut brown, the very colour of the mushrooms I was eating.

This is the hunter-gatherer way.

Beautiful seaweed walk today with two wonderful women, thank you Gita and Anna. May wild food protect you, entertain you, love you and nourish you, always x

Out alone at the edge of the sea today, the Autumn Equinox's full Moon had pulled the tide out as far as it will go this year and had exposed places not glimpsed since the Equinox in Spring.

The seaweed I found around these magical pools was more bountiful than any I'd seen and as I clipped the Carrageen Moss from rocks simply bulging with it, I realised that it was much like gardening. My pruning would help the plants for next year. This must have been the very first garden we tended.

I felt so happy doing it, sun shining, water glinting, pottering in my sea garden.

I'm very glad I wasn't actually *in* the rock pool because there was a sudden thrash behind me. Something pretty big was in there. And then I saw it: a 2.5 foot dogfish (shark family), thrashing at the Kelp and launching itself onto the raised ledge of rock that separated it from the sea. It kept having to thrash itself back into the pool again; then swam lazily around.

At one point it came straight towards me, looking at me, then turned and in the swish of its tail caused the surface to explode in a mass of sunlight shimmers so I couldn't see it anymore. Again it launched itself onto the Kelp and had to wriggle back down again. This time when it swam towards me I really got the impression it was saying "Look, that's where I normally get out but I can't now. Do *you* know the way out?"

And then I realised what had happened: he didn't know that this would be the lowest tide of the year and so the channel he'd normally use was no longer under the water.

I thought for a moment that if he launched himself back up onto the Kelp ledge I might try and push him towards the sea but remembering there's a tooth on every scale of its hide so it feels like sandpaper, not to mention the ones in his mouth, I thought better to let the tide come in and lift him gently out.

This is might not be the hunter-gatherer way but it seemed like the best idea at the time.

If you start feeling depressed at this time of year, you might be interested in the following idea of what to focus on:

The ratio of equal daylight and darkness at the Autumn Equinox causes special receptors in our eyes to send a message to our Pineal gland. This message: that winter is on its way, causes the Pineal gland to start releasing melatonin into our blood.

Melatonin is the hormone that makes us want to sleep and it will be increased as the nights grow longer. But in the small doses released at the Autumn Equinox, it simply gives us the urge to begin the gathering-in process.

If we heed its instructions to gather what we need, it will lead us to a winter where our cupboards are full of delicious foods, our warm clothes and boots are in good order, and, if we are lucky enough to have a fire, our storage places are full of good dry wood and kindling. So, it gives us something practical to focus on and so we have used Nature's power upon us to our benefit.

By being fully prepared, we can be fully relaxed and so we can fully enjoy the true magnificence of being clever.

This is how all the wild animals are responding to their shots of melatonin.

This is the hunter-gatherer way.

Such a wonderful review from a young mother who is now half-way through the book:

"I need to tell you that "The Hunter-Gatherer Way" may be one of my favourite books already! The way you write is beautiful and so engaging, but also what you have written is so perfect and spot on that I resonate with it so deeply. If only everyone could read this book it might just save the world! Not only from the point of view of gathering food, but the insight into ourselves and how lost humanity is.

I love it, I love your book and the spark it has ignited in me and my partner to trust our instincts and nature. It makes so much sense. I could honestly go on and on about how amazing it is, but I had better not!

Many thanks
Annabelle xx"

I was just thinking about how you mustn't gather wild mushrooms from beside a busy road because they absorb the fumes and store them. So then I thought: without a road they'll still be absorbing whatever's in the air and storing it too.

What's in the air in wild places?

An elixir of pheromones emitted by all the plants and the trees and the passing wild animals.

This is the hunter-gatherer way.

There is a very simple way of adding wild fruit to autumnal cooking which requires no sugar or topping and tailing, and which tastes so good it will lift your spirits even on the dullest of days.

The flavours are so rich and so exciting because the wild berries are simply powerhouses of the perfect nutrients to fortify our blood, preparing our bodies for the winter.

All you have to do is to take a basket and go out to the cleanest, wildest places you know and gather a gleaming mixture of wild Rosehips, Rowanberries, Blackberries, Haws, Sloes and Crab Apples.

It's impossible to find these wild berries without smiling. Every time you spot them in the hedgerow, your heart will give a sudden jolt of joy and as you gather them into your basket, especially those above your head, you'll probably find that you're laughing.

Picking bright orange berries out of clear blue skies gives your mind a feast of zinging colour that stays with you even when you close your eyes to go to sleep.

These contrasting colours activate the rods and cones at the back of your eyes making it easier for you to spot the berries the next time you go out hunting for them.

There's no need to top and tail, just wash them by holding the basket under a tap, allowing the water to run through the basket like a colander. (A willow basket will love this treatment because it needs the water to remain healthy; then hang it up to dry.)

Smash the Rosehips in a pestle and mortar and then put all the berries together in a large saucepan, cover with boiling water to three times the height and bring back to the boil. Reduce the heat and simmer for 25 minutes, stirring occasionally.

If you have Rosehips in the mixture you *must* use muslin (or a clean drying-up cloth doubled) during the straining process because Rosehips contains tiny hairs which can irritate or puncture the stomach. If you don't have any Rosehips in the mix you can just use a normal sieve to strain off the fruit pulp from the liquid.

The resulting clear liquid is what you want: a deep red/purple wild fruit stock which contains all the vitamins and minerals you need.

Don't worry about the effects of the simmering on the quality and quantity of the nutrients, the M.O.D. ran some tests on Rosehips during the war to see if they would be a good source of Vitamin C instead of oranges. They tested the Vitamin C before and after 6 hours of boiling and found there was virtually no change if the berries had been put into *boiling* water and not into cold water.

Use it as the base for soups, casseroles, fruit crumbles, porridge or have it has a hot drink, diluted, with a little honey added. I know this will sound like sacrilege but it's so fabulous I had to mention it, if you stir in a couple of tablespoonfuls of Bisto into the boiling wild fruit stock it is *heavenly* poured over roast vegetables. You can also marinade meat with it and it will break down the fibres making even the toughest of venison into the food of the gods.

This nourishing stock will last you about a week by which time you'll be longing to go out and gather some more berries. You now have the perfect excuse. See what using sugar as a preservative has robbed us of?

This is the hunter-gatherer way.

If you want a beautiful complexion just go for a walk in the rain. This is the hunter-gatherer way.

I gave a copy of "The Hunter-Gatherer Way" to a woman who has lived on Dartmoor all her life. She's nearly 70 now and she was taught the old ways of the moor by her mother and her grandmother before her. I held my breath. A nod of approval from her would really let me know I'd found something.

A few days later, she rang me to say that she'd tried to read it while at home but just couldn't get into it so she'd taken it up to the moor and read the whole thing in one go while sitting outside.

When she'd finished reading, she said she looked up and looked around her and "the moor suddenly came alive as I'd never seen it before".

There was so much delight in her voice as she told me that it lit me up inside as well and we spent the next few moments just laughing and laughing.

This is the hunter-gatherer way.

There is a saying round here that "You mustn't eat the blackberries after 1st October because then the Devil pees on them".

I wonder if it's because after this a lot of blackberries have begun to ferment and so are slightly alcoholic. Wanting to ward off children we called that alcohol "the Devil's pee"?

I've just had an amazing experience with an optical illusion that I've never noticed before.

Standing on the bank of the River Dart, watching the leaves flying along, twisting and turning under the surface of the water, I heard a massive splash and caught sight of the tail end of a fish.

I wanted to be ready for the next jump so I used an optical trick I'd been taught years ago by a hunter to detect movement:

Stare straight ahead of you at a fixed point and then be aware of what's in the peripherals of your vision without moving your eyes.

Suddenly even the tiniest of movements become more obvious. Then you can move your eyes to it to see what it is.

You've no doubt seen rabbits and sheep and deer doing this as they look towards you but don't quite seem to be looking *at* you. They do it for the same reason: to detect movement, to try and work out whether you're there or not.

I used to think it very unfair that when deer sensed I was there but couldn't see me they would reassure themselves there was nothing to worry about and carry on grazing. So, I used to waive at them. They can see movement which goes from side to side (no doubt the origin of the waive) but not movement that's from something moving towards them which is why it's possible to stalk them.

The first three occasions I saw them and waived they jumped and run away but, the fourth time I did it, they didn't run; they just looked at me waiving and carried on grazing. By breaking my cover with such a strong gesture, I think they knew I wasn't trying to trick them, so they trusted me and I got to watch them for ages.

But this morning, standing very still, letting the river's movement flood into my peripherals, waiting for any movement that could be the beginnings of a great leap from a mighty fish, I got bored and decided to look up at something moving in the trees above the river.

As I did so, I realised that the trees were moving very strangely. There was no wind but they were swaying to the right and wouldn't come back to the left. I felt sick and as though I was going to fall over. Then I realised that my eyes had caused a juxtaposition of movement by laying the movement of the fast running river over the still, straight trees, it was causing the trees to look like *they* were flowing.

I wonder what this will be useful for?

This is the hunter-gatherer way.

A wonderful day yesterday along the banks of the mighty River Dart with a group of hunter-gatherers and berries, nuts, roots, wild mushrooms, lichens and cooling breezes.

So much chattering laughter that if I'd closed my eyes I'd have felt transported back to central Africa with the Pygmy women.

I'm sure that chattering laughter is the sound that humans are meant to make.

And then to be given a beautiful woollen coat, hand made for me by Annabel of Avalon Elf Coats in the colours of the Highlands and Islands of Scotland. I will treasure this coat and wear it to disappear into the woods so that the birds don't screech at me and I can hear them make their own sounds of chattering laughter.

This is the hunter-gatherer way.

A note I made after giving a talk about "The Hunter-Gatherer Way" in Totnes:

Having worked on my own all these years, being guided simply by my hunches and the soul shuddering that would go on to let me know I'd found something, I never really knew if it was just my fancy.

But as the talk progressed last night, I realised the audience were experiencing these incredible moments too. There was such a stillness in the air and as one of them said later, "It was like having a wave pass over me".

When I got home there was a message from another:

"It was amazing to feel the jigsaw coming together as you spoke, I felt so inspired and my mind expanded. I walked home feeling excited and smiling all the way x" *Sula Blight*

Now that I really know I have found something good, I want to do as the Cherokee grandmother said in Forrest Carter's book "The Education of Little Tree" and pass it on.

So thank you to the audience for following your hunches and coming to the talk, thank you for allowing yourselves to be opened, for riding those incredible feelings of illumination, and for your silent pledges to share it with whosoever you can find.

This is the hunter-gatherer way.

A wonderful group of people from the organisation "Explorers Connect" came on a wild food walk yesterday.

Along the River Dart we looked at berries, nuts, roots, lichen and fungi and then in the evening I went over to their lodgings to give a talk and we lit candles and turned out the electric light and drank mugs of the wild fruit stock they'd made with the day's gatherings.

I told them stories from the desert and the rainforest and the moor, and the Moon shone and the stars twinkled and by the warmth of their smiles in the glow of the candle-light I felt that magical seeds were growing in fertile ground.

This is the hunter-gatherer way.

We've just moved into a 400 year old cottage. On the night of the full Moon, I went up into the attic and found a tiny window made of thick, uneven glass.

I tried to find the Moon through the glass but the irregularities kept distorting the light so that I had to sway about to gather the light together to make a whole Moon. It looked very small and far away.

Satisfied that I could get it all in focus, I decided to let it go and look into the light on the glass's distorted edges to see what would happen there. I managed to get a huge amount of it together and when I looked into it, and got it in focus, I realised I was looking at the craters on its surface.

Once I'd recovered from the excitement, I wondered what the moonbeams were doing. It took me a while to locate them because I was actually sitting on them. As I studied them from the side of the attic, I realised the glass had gathered them and shaped them into what looked exactly like a campfire.

The light didn't flicker though, it just held its shape; a silver fire cast silently across the floor of the attic of this ancient cottage and the stillness and magic of it almost made me cry.

This is the hunter-gatherer way.

So lovely to hear about an adventure from someone who came on a seaweed walk with me in the summer: last week she went back to the shore to gather a small supply of brown seaweeds for the winter.

Once she'd filled her basket, she noticed the water in the rock pools looked very inviting so she thought she'd just have a quick dip to see what it would be like. It was so deliciously life-affirming that she just started laughing and laughing and thinking "This is the life!"

This is the hunter-gatherer way.

I often think that what really separates us from our hunter-gatherer selves isn't 4,000 years, but about half an inch of shoe leather.

Wrapped and bound, our feet have become so ultra sensitive that we believe the ground is awful.

It takes awakening an even deeper belief, that we are made for this land, to take them off and set our feet free, and then it doesn't take long for them to find their way. The feelings they give us from the leaves and earth and warm puddles, is the loving we've hungered for all these years.

And as with any kind of relationship, you take the rough with the smooth.

This is the hunter-gatherer way.

Last night, I made the wild fruit stock by candle-light. I wanted to know what would happen to the colours.

After turning off the electric light, the berries I lifted out and held up to the flame were just boring looking and dulled by the steam of cooking angels that danced up from the pot.

As I kept stirred gently, a sleepy feeling began to come over me and it must have been a good half an hour later just as I was beginning to think it must be cooked by now, when I realised the colours had changed. They were now so very, very beautiful. And I realised that it wasn't the cooking that had changed them from being dull to being magical: it was the candle light's gradual effect on my eyes.

Our eyes are not designed to see magical colours by electric light, but they *are* designed to see them by the light of the fire.

This is the hunter-gatherer way.

Amazing culinary discovery yesterday: I took some dried wild mushrooms (Ceps, Brown Birch Bolete, Hedgehog Fungus and The Blusher) and reconstituted them before cooking but instead of using water, I soaked them in wild fruit stock that I'd made out of Rosehips, Haws, Sloes, Guelder Rose, Rowan and Crab Apple. Then I cooked the mushrooms in the stock with some roots.

The flavours lifted me so high I felt like I was singing with angels. This special dish, taking a long time to prepare, is definitely a celebration food.

Knowing what to gather is one thing but knowing what to *bring together* takes us to new doors to step into whole new worlds.

This is the hunter-gatherer way.

Every connection you make with Nature is actually a door.
This is the hunter-gatherer way.

A lovely message from someone who had read "The Hunter-Gatherer Way" then came on a Berries, Nuts, Roots, Lichen & Fungi walk last week:

"Thank you Ffyona for gently guiding us into the embrace of Mother Earth and opening our senses to the abundance of nourishment all around us in the wild…a transformational experience!" *Maya Melrose*

This is the hunter-gatherer way.

I lost my footing whilst out mushrooming on Dartmoor and was about to fall backwards down a very long, steep slope when I managed to grab at a spindly looking beech tree branch and pull myself to safety, headfirst into the leaf-litter and grass at the almost vertical base of the tree.

Shaking a bit from the shock, still lying flat on my face against the vertical bank, I was just thanking that fine beech branch for its amazing strength when I realised that right by my face, camouflaged amongst the shadows of the wet brown leaves was one of the most difficult to find and most delicious of all the wild mushrooms: The Horn of Plenty. And plenty of 'em!

This is the hunter-gatherer way.

A group I took out on Saturday for an autumn wild food walk were really amazing, over half of them taking a leap of faith and going barefoot with me, despite the cold. They went through some really significant pain thresholds, breaking through to the other side. One of them sent me this email afterwards:

"Hi Ffyona

Just wanted to let you know how much I enjoyed your walk today! Such a sensory experience: taste, touch, sight, information in a magical tale and spirituality! Thank you for taking me out of my comfort zone into something invigorating and natural! I can't wait to come on another walk!" *Kate x*

This is the hunter-gatherer way.

This is a message for Lee who came to the talk tonight: you had a copy of my book "The Whole Story" with you, it was well worn, the cover's stiffness creased into softness and it was held deeply in the crook of your arm.

I thought about it all the way home, the briefness of the meeting and wished I'd spent longer with you. I find the pace of signings hard to navigate sometimes; the line of people waiting often keeps me from being able to meet each person as deeply as I want to.

I just wanted to say, Lee, that I'm not sure I've ever seen such a beautiful copy of the book.

When Elsa was still little, and I told her the trees were falling asleep now for the winter, she asked if I thought they would like a lullaby? She wanted the trees to be assured that no harm would come to them while they slept and so we adapted the words of a Christmas Carol.

Then I put her in a sling on my back and we walked through the woods singing it to them. You'll know the tune, and it went like this:

"And the wind will rock you, rock you, rock you,
And the wind will rock you, rock you, rock you.
Feel the earth beneath your feet,
Snugly round your roots so deep.

And the rain will wash you, wash you, wash you,
And the rain will wash you, wash you, wash you.
Feel the earth beneath your feet,
Snugly round your roots so deep.

And the Sun will dry you, dry you, dry you,
And the Sun will dry you, dry you, dry you.
Feel the earth beneath your feet,
Snugly round your roots so deep.

And the Moon will guide you, guide, you, guide you,
And the Moon will guide you, guide, you, guide you,
Feel the earth beneath your feet,
Snugly round your roots so deep.

And we will sing to you, sing to you, sing to you,
And we will sing to you, sing to you, sing to you.
Feel the earth beneath your feet,
Snugly round your roots so deep."

Over and over again until all the trees were asleep, and Elsa too. This is the hunter-gatherer way.

Between now and mid-winter, the light will grow richer and richer every day.

It pours out across the landscape like syrup of sunlight.

It is the highest quality light of the year and getting more concentrated by the day.

It's as though the night is *compressing* the light and making it the most beautiful that it can ever be.

And at the mid-winter sunrise, when the sun "stands still" and rises from the same point for four days in a row, the light will be so intense it will look like liquid gold.

I think that the journey to drink of this, the most golden light after the longest night, is the ultimate destination of winter.

This is the hunter-gatherer way.

There is a massive endorphin high to be had, to fill the whole being with multiple explosions of joy, and it's just over the top of every good hill and goes far deeper than any amount of view.

Yet it so often goes unnoticed. We've been taught to stop at the top and congratulate ourselves on being the King of the Castle. But, Nature doesn't reward us with her greatest pleasures when the ego is involved.

So to get this kind of bliss, you have to go further, you have to go a bit *further* than the top of the hill.

It all starts by choosing a decent sized hill and starting out slowly until you are walking evenly and strongly up the hill. Your heart will be thumping powerfully, your breathing will be deep and regular, your mind will be opened and relaxed, your muscles will be relaxed when the burning gets too great so the blood can flow freely, your sweat will be pulsing and so all of you is working hard and in balance.

When you can see you're getting close to the top, *speed up*. Take your mind off the sight of it and concentrate instead on the feeling in your thighs. You'll know when you've got to the top because the burning will suddenly cease but your heart and lungs will be thumping at full pelt making your legs go faster and faster as though you're about to fly.

At this point hold your breath in and don't let it out for 6 good strides at full pelt over the top of the hill.

You'll feel like you're simply bursting with brightness, stride after stride after stride.

This is the hunter-gatherer way.

Before every wild food walk we gather together in a ring, hold hands, close our eyes and say a blessing.

It was something I learned to do from a seaweed gatherer in Cornwall, Rory MacPhee, and it's become such an important part of the walk and it ends the walk too. The blessing I use goes like this:

Blessings on the blossom,
Blessings on the fruit,
Blessings on the leaf and stem,
And blessings on the root.

Recently, I've realised that it has another meaning. I realised that it isn't just about the wild food, it's also about our journey of learning.

Elsa once noticed that ideas grow in the same way as plants. A seed is sown, it begins to take root, and as it grows stronger it begins to bear fruit.

This is the hunter-gatherer way.

Standing high on the edge of Dartmoor and watching the water vapour rising up from the river valley, I suddenly realised something: evaporation doesn't just lift the water, it *purifies* it too.

What a clever system! The world can now be washed in *pure* water.

When we are taught about the world at school it is through separate subjects that never link up so, is it hardly surprising that people feel disconnected from Nature when they are not taught in Geography that evaporation *purifies* the water as well as lifting it up to make clouds?

If we join the dots, the true wonders of the world will be revealed.

This is the hunter-gatherer way.

On the Spring Wild Food Walk last Saturday, I noticed something pretty amazing about what happens to people when they suddenly spot something they're looking for: they jump.

It's like getting a shot of electricity and it has the effect of instantly waking people up because they suddenly become much more present; another way of getting people out of their heads and into the reality of the moment.

And then I realised that this feeling never goes away, in fact the more you know about wild food, the more often and the more intensely it happens. It's like being jump started into a higher state of wakefulness every few minutes, all through the day.

Perhaps this is what electricity is really for. No wonder we feel so dead without wild food.

This is the hunter-gatherer way.

Everyone's commenting on how well Elsa and I look right now and we definitely feel amazing. So, as we're only eating wild food for our greens, I thought I'd do a nutritional comparison between edible wild leaves and organic lettuce.

The results were amazing - wild food has at least double the quantity of vitamins and minerals than farmed food:

THE NUTRITION OF WILD FOOD vs. ORGANIC LETTUCE

Lettuce..........500 I.U. of Vitamin A
Dock Leaf......12,900 I.U. of Vitamin A
Lettuce..........0.9mg of iron
Nettle...........1.6mg of iron
Lettuce..........18mg of Vitamin C
Dock Leaf......119mg of Vitamin C
Lettuce..........1.4g protein
Wild Garlic....6.2g protein
Lettuce..........40mg calcium
Dandelion.....187mg calcium
Lettuce..........30mg phosphorous
Wild Garlic....202mg phosphorous

Lettuce………..0.07mg Thiamine
Wild Garlic…..0.25mg Thiamine
Lettuce………...0.08mg Riboflavin
Wild Fennel…..0.15mg Riboflavin
This is the hunter-gatherer way.

On a wild food walk recently, one of the participants told me a story about when he was invited to go hunting with some Bushmen in Namibia. As they followed the tracks of the antelope, the Bushmen told him they could tell which of the herd were pregnant and just how pregnant they were.

Then he said something even more amazing: they told him the lions can tell this too.

But here in the modern world, in our urgency to make journeys quicker, we have covered the paths in tarmac and forgotten how important it is to gather the news along the way. If only we knew what had happened in the hours preceding us, if only we had been able to see the signs and piece things together and made sense of them *before* we got somewhere, we would feel more comfortable arriving and there might be fewer misunderstandings between us.

And we wouldn't look at the tarmac paths and in seeing nothing, think we are the only animals left on Earth.

This is the hunter-gatherer way.

Have you ever noticed how firelight makes older people look young again?

This is the hunter-gatherer way.

Looking at seagulls flying just for the sheer bliss of it, I realised this is what they do to relax their muscles and unwind their minds after the tension and concentration of hunting.

Listening to cats purring, I realise it's for the same reason.

So, what do humans do?

We don't play on the wind, we don't purr......in order to unwind after hunting and gathering, we *dance*.

This is the hunter-gatherer way.

A review from Tim "Mac" Macartney, founder of Embercombe, a very special outdoor education centre in Devon:

"I felt and appreciated the deep sensitivity, respect, and dignity with which you drew us into the mystery and truth of this most beautiful 'way'.

I am reading your book "The Hunter-Gatherer Way", but slowly, relishing the many miles and long silences that gave you access to the insights that yielded this knowledge. It's not a long read, but your book is packed with information, insight, and wisdom. More than that.... it feels to me that you have accomplished something quite startling and of enormous potential for our numbed and somewhat saddened 'civilised' society.

I found our Spring Wild Food Walk together nourishing and life-affirming, a continuing homeward bound journey."

This is the hunter-gatherer way.

This time last year I suddenly realised why birds sing the dawn chorus. The sound is *so loud*, I'd thought, how can they make such a big sound? They must have very big lungs.

Why would little birds need such big lungs?

What are lungs? They're bags of air in the chest. Would having big ones rather than little ones help them to fly? Yes! It would be like having two large balloons inside them.

So what would *singing* do to these balloons? Singing would fill them up with *warm air*, making them even more *boyant*.

And so, by singing the dawn chorus, the birds are getting their lungs ready for a day of flight. And every time they land on a branch during the day and sing, it's like they're stopping at a petrol station and filling them up again.

This is the hunter-gatherer way.

For really brightened days, naturally, just put edible wild plants into a teapot, pour on water that's just off boiling, let infuse and drink it all through the day.

This is the hunter-gatherer way.

One of the women I really admire and look up to in the journey of re-discovering our lost knowledge, is Glennie Kindred, author and artist.

So, I sent her a copy of "The Hunter-Gatherer Way" and waited with baited breath.....Here's what she said:

"I LOVE it!! and haven't been able to put it down, it is just wonderful.... I'm loving all your insights about our relationship to the land and our separation from nature.... which fascinates me too..... and so loving your insights based on your experiences living with the aboriginal people.....

Much Love and appreciation!" Glennie
Wow!!

Some people think there are no wild plants in Britain poisonous enough to kill you.

On one of my Spring Wild Food Walks recently, I was told of a young man who had taken a fancy to a thick, bushy plant that looks like wild celery or flat leafed parsley. So, he put a handful into his soup.

And after eating it he went into a coma.

The hospital didn't expect him to come out of it.

After 3 days and 3 nights he finally began to regain consciousness. Any more of it and he'd have died.

What had he eaten? Hemlock Water Dropwort.

It's one of the most poisonous plants on Earth and it grows in abundance in Britain. It has leaves like Hawthorn leaves which grow in branches from a central stem, like a Christmas tree, and it does look a lot like celery.

So, if you feel the call of the wild this spring and want to go gathering wild food, please be sure of what you're experimenting with. Man might have killed all the dangerous wild animals on our island but he couldn't stop the dangerous plants from popping up behind him.

This is the hunter-gatherer way.

On my wild food walks, I'm often asked whether I hunt animals as well as gather wild plants.

"No," I say, "I don't hunt animals. I consider that to be a man's job."

This answer always causes a stir, especially from the women, which is understandable when you consider our history.

The men though, don't *say* anything at all.

They respond by suddenly appearing much taller, and their shoulders suddenly look much broader and yet more relaxed. Their expressions seem more gentle and they have a calmness about them as if from an inner knowing, without even a hint of ego or arrogance. It's really quite a beautiful transformation to watch. Suddenly (and forgive me for saying this) they look like *men*.

I came to the conclusion that hunting animals is a man's job after asking many men who had killed animals how they coped with dealing the death blow. All of them used the same word: "just".

They said: "Well, you just bop them on the head or wring their neck." That word "just" made me realise something different happens for them in that moment than happens for many women.

Generally speaking, I think that men naturally find it easier than women do to disconnect their emotions from their actions and so they can "just" bop them on the head.

Women, on the other hand, need to keep their emotions with them in crisis moments so that we can put ourselves into the shoes of those we are caring for to work out what it is they need in order to feel better. If we disconnected our emotions at the moment the baby is screaming its hardest, it would be all too easy to "just" bop it on the head.

Being able to disconnect and being unable to disconnect are equally important. Neither can do it all alone. So, we need each other's special qualities, and, if given half the chance, we are often simply amazed by each other. And so we have equal respect.

I know that for many generations, women have had to fight against the male ego and I'm so grateful they did, it was out of control. But now we are in danger of losing a place for men altogether, requiring that they get in touch with their feminine side all the time and not allowing them to disconnect.

I know this idea might bring a string of indignant comments about how I can't generalise, but, if you had seen the beautiful transformation that took place after I had honoured the men, you too would think it's worth taking that risk.

This is the hunter-gatherer way.

The last of the Spring Wild Food Walks takes place tomorrow (before the seaweed walks begin) and, as always, I look back on the season and think about how much I have learned.

So much of my coal-face now is about how *others* learn.

I used to allow a free flow of questions and contributions on the walks but I came to see that those who ask the most questions are often the ones who don't listen to the answers and don't learn anything new. They can also be an annoyance to others and, to my cost, I've found there is no polite way of shutting them up once they've started!

So, I wondered what the Aborigines would do in this situation?

I remembered hearing that Aboriginal children between the ages of 9 and 11 are not allowed to speak at all. This is the age when children ask the most questions and don't listen to the answers.

So, I applied this rule to the walks for adults too, and it worked. And, as always happens when tapping into the right kind of tool, unexpected things started to happen, magical things.

A natural peace would immediately descend on the group. Why? Because suddenly everyone would feel safe. Without speech no one is vying to be the cleverest; no one is worrying about showing how little they know; no one is worrying about having to make small talk with complete strangers; no one is getting frustrated with the constant interruptions and wanting to just wring someone's neck.

Without speech, people unite. And in that harmony, their minds begin to open. It feels like being within a great, sweet, open pool that simply fills with wonder.

This is the hunter-gatherer way.

The first Seaweed Wild Food Walk of the year took place last Saturday and we had a wonderful time.

The seaweed was pretty wonderful too, quite startling in fact. It is more plump and more luscious this year than I have *ever* seen it before.

Why would that be?

I put this conundrum to the group and we all recalled the strange weather we've had over the winter of *huge* amounts of rain. Could this be the cause of the wildly abundant seaweed? But how would *rainwater* affect seaweed?

It didn't obviously make sense and as nothing else came to mind, I left the mystery there, letting it simmer at the back of my mind to find its own connections. By taking my eye off a problem, I often find that the answer comes into my head whilst doing something completely different, sometimes many years later.

Luckily however, I worked this one out quite quickly. I remembered a moment when, during a break in the rainstorms this winter, I was standing on the cliff path looking out into the sea. I was looking out to sea rather than looking down at the mud on the path because something out there had caught my eye.

The sea was a very strange colour: it was completely *opaque*. It was like blue/green milk. Why would that be? I'd wondered at the time. And then I'd realised it must be because the rainstorms had washed down the nutrients from the river banks and all of it had flooded out to sea. And this had been going on day after day, for weeks.

I remember thinking "I bet we're going to have some very big fish this year". And then, a few weeks later, someone had told me he'd found hundreds of clams on a beach where he'd never seen clams before and I'd thought it must have been the nutrients washed down the rivers from the rainstorms.

So, here we are a few months later, finding the richest abundance of seaweed I have ever seen. It would make perfect sense then, that the seaweed must also be improved by all those nutrients.

So, you could say that a wet winter means a bumper crop of seaweed.

This is the hunter-gatherer way.

This beautiful review arrived in my mailbox......

"Out of the corner of my eye, I can see "The Hunter-Gatherer Way" poking out of the envelope that it arrived in from my dear friends in Buckfastleigh. It has been read and re-read and put back in the envelope to keep it pristine. I feel a shiver go down my spine as I notice it and remember that feeling that I got when I first finished it, like finding that I wasn't alone, or stupid or worthless any more. As if I had found the thread that takes me from this, this mess that we have made back to a time when it wasn't so messy, and in doing so, forward to a time when it won't be so messy again. I see through different eyes now, everything from people playing on the beach, to my children, to my love, and am more at peace knowing what I know, what you have shown me, so carefully and graciously, and without guile. You have tapped me gently on the shoulder and whispered into my ear, "Look over here, I think this is what you are looking for" and d'you know what, I think you're right! Thank you, Ffyona..." Simon Medhurst

This is the hunter-gatherer way.

I was lying on the beach today after gathering seaweed and I pulled my hair over my eyes to see what the sun looks like through its strands. After a few minutes I noticed something I've never seen before - my hair is full of rainbows.

This is the hunter-gatherer way.

During those really hot days, I took to swimming in the river to cool down. But, being a solitary kind of animal, I went later. At dusk. When there was nobody else around.

As I swam in the fading light, I noticed there were thousands of mosquitoes just bobbing up and down on the surface and that my head was actually gathering them.

Just as I was wondering whether this blissful swim was about to turn into a blood bath of mosquito bites on my warm scalp, a bat swooped down and ate some of them. And then another bat came. And another. And another.

And as I swam down the river through the deepening dusk, a hat of tiny dancing wings with fluttering black leather bows was merrily whirling about my head.

This is the hunter-gatherer way.

Many years ago when Elsa was learning how to swim in the river, we discovered a magical way of pushing through that initial barrier of "It's going to be *so* cold in there!" in order to get into the water.

First, you ease yourself in up to your waist and wait until you feel relaxed. Then if, with one great, determined gesture, you push yourself in with your hands out in front of you and at the same time you call out in a clear, steady voice "Hello the River!", a few firm, strong, breast strokes later, you will feel *warm*. And it will feel as though the river has brought you a fur coat.

Elsa believed this so strongly after a summer of finding out how well it works that when winter came she decided that if she just shouted "Hello the River!" no matter how cold the water was, the river would bring her a fur coat. I warmed her up very quickly by the fire as soon as she realised what actually happens.

This is the hunter-gatherer way.

Here's a funny thing that happened today after delicious hours spent gathering Carrageen Moss seaweed. This plant is often covered in what look like electric blue lights when it's submerged in rock pools. The "lights" are the pure oxygen that it has extracted from the water and when you lift the seaweed out of the water, they go out and when you put it back in, they go on again.

But the seaweed I was gathering today had no lights on it at all because I didn't want to take it from the rock pools but from the dry, exposed rocks where it has to produce more gel in order to keep it from drying out in the sun; and it was the *gel* in this seaweed that I wanted.

After a couple of hours my basket was full so I sat down on the edge of the sea and closed my eyes. Of course, all I could see behind my eye lids was the Carrageen Moss scene, now in hues of red and brown - as often happens when you've been concentrating on one kind of thing and then close your eyes.

And then I wondered what would happen if I tilted my head upwards and let the sun shine on my closed eye lids…it was *so* beautiful: the sunlight had turned on all the blue lights.

This is the hunter-gatherer way.

At a recent talk I gave, the gardeners in the audience were rather angry that I said edible wild plants are healthier and more nutritious than cultivated plants.

Having given this some further thought, I don't think gardeners realise that every plant has evolved to do various jobs in the eco-system. And even if they did consider this, what arrogance to presume they know those jobs better than the plant and can therefore put them in exactly the right place.

If *you* are forced to live somewhere where someone else has put you, where you can't do the job you were born to do, where every aspect of your life is dictated by someone who doesn't even know you have a job to do, are you really going to be healthier and happier than those who are free to choose?

I actually got the impression that the gardeners felt the plants should be grateful to them!

This is the hunter-gatherer way.

There's a little job we are designed to do in Nature which helps to make sure there's wild food for tomorrow and which most of us aren't even aware of and are most likely not doing properly at all.

Last autumn I realised why prunes (dried plums) give us loose stools. I'd noticed that wild plums had given a Badger them too, right beside the tree.

Why would that be?

I'd looked at the tree and saw that it was at the end of a long row of wild plum trees and I'd looked at the loose Badger droppings all full of seeds and I'd suddenly realised why: wild plum trees likes to grow with other wild plum trees in a long line, no doubt for its protection or for cross-pollination of male and female plants. So, it has developed a fruit which gives the eater the runs and makes them drop the seeds close to the tree.

I was telling this to some people on one of my wild food walks recently and someone added that Acacia trees in the Sahara desert have the opposite effect, giving the eater constipation. Which of course would make perfect sense: an Acacia tree does not want another Acacia tree growing right beside it and competing for water and so it ensures that the barer of its seeds is a long way off before dropping them.

This is the hunter-gatherer way.

A wild food walk is not just a door to Nature, and to freedom, it's also the doorway to magic.

This is the hunter-gatherer way.

Some people measure their wild mushroom haul by its weight, but I think I've found a better way: 134 moments of pure delight in half an afternoon.

This is the hunter-gatherer way.

I am working for the biggest organism on Earth.

Torn at, stung, scratched, slung into bogs, into cobwebs with massive spiders in, hair pulled out by thorns - what could make anyone *want* to do this, for hours and hours on end?

Mushrooms.

And after I'd found a basket full of the finest and had gone home and eaten them, in bliss, in pure, unadulterated (whatever that means) luxurious *heavenly bliss*, three days of violent "wind" have followed. It was *so* violent that I've had to stop and wonder: why would that be?

And then I'd realised - the mycelium that has created these mushrooms and has lured me into hunting for them and feasting on them has turned me into a massively dynamic disperser of spores with every gust of violent "wind" I make.

This is the hunter-gatherer way.

How does it serve the mushroom to have so much magic in it? Because people will pick the magic ones and leave the other ones behind.

This is the hunter-gatherer way.

On a wild food walk recently, I led a group of adults to a Beech tree and showed them how to find the small triangular seed cases which contain the edible Beechnut.

Very quickly they'd abandoned all cares and troubles from beyond the tree to be completely focused on finding its treasure.

After a while I'd called out to them that they seemed so happy there, maybe I should just leave them to enjoy themselves rather than look at the rest of the things I was going to show them. A big part of them agreed, I knew they just wanted to stay there, where they were like children again, where they'd found what they were really looking for.

And then I thought of the 34,000 children who had called Childline last year with thoughts of suicide. And I wished those children could just find their way to a Beech tree where under the great, protecting arms of its mighty branches, all children become free of their fears and worries, free to just scamp about amongst the golden leaves, hunting for triangles of sweet pleasure.

This is the hunter-gatherer way.

"Why do you look at the Moon?" I posted on my Facebook page. So many people commented and the theme was all the same: it's because of a *love* for the Moon. A love that isn't like any other.

The light of the Moon actually helps to regulate our hormones. It triggers a receptor in our eyes which sends a message to the Pineal gland to release different hormones at different times of the year.

Our bodies need these hormones in the right doses at the right times so that we have our babies in the spring, so that we conceive in the summer, so that everything we need will be available to us at the right time of year in our cycle of birth, maturity, procreation and death.

We're biologically designed to look at the Moon. We feel it as love. And *love* is how Nature gets us to do everything.

This is the hunter-gatherer way.

So, the shortest day and the longest night are upon us. If it's clear, there'll be magic out there under the stars tonight and many living things will die.

A couple of years ago, a friend and I made a fire on the beach, we wrapped ourselves in blankets and we lay down on sheepskins beside it. We lay on our backs and we looked up at the firmament, for hours and hours and hours.

We were aware that the top of the Earth had tipped the furthest away from the Sun that it ever goes and so the northern horizon was revealing stars that are only seen there for these few nights of the Winter Solstice. Like the rock pools and caverns that I glimpse only twice a year at the two lowest tides (at the new Moon after the Equinoxes), the stars we saw there were the rarest of the sky-diamonds, appearing only at the lowest of the sky-tides. So, we said "Hello the stars!"

People often say that when they look up at the stars they feel so small and insignificant. I don't feel like that. I feel that if I can see the light of a star, the light of that star can see me. I have been seen by the light of Mars and Venus and Jupiter and Saturn, by the light of the Andromeda galaxy, by all the lights of Orion and by the lights of millions of stars I'll never know the names of. I have also been seen by the light of stars that no longer exist. Knowing this makes me feel amazing.

All through the night, we felt a powerful sensation raining down on us, a massive kind of energy that felt rich and right and pure and good and we soaked ourselves in it. And we made wishes.

Looking back on it now, 3 or 4 years later, I realise we were probably soaking up the cosmic rays which had come from stars exploding half-way across the galaxy a million years ago; and that all but one of the wishes I made that night has now come true.

This is the hunter-gatherer way.

Have you ever wondered where New Year comes from?

Why is it now? Why is it celebrated in the dark? Why not later, when it starts to get lighter and we've had a little bit longer in bed?

I've often wondered about this too but it was only yesterday that I suddenly realised the answer.

The two winter celebrations of Christmas and New Year are ancient. Of course, as many people will know, when Christianity first forced itself onto the British Isles (apparently in the bloodiest conversion of any country in Europe because we resisted it so strongly), the Winter Solstice celebration was replaced by Christmas.

But, what was the New Year celebration a replacement of? Or is New Year just a modern construct to get us back into harness more quickly whilst also getting us to make personal promises to enjoy ourselves less and to work even harder?

I think the clue to what New Year once was, is by asking what New Year *actually* is…

New Year might be the time we reflect on our deeds (no bad thing of course), and the time we make personal promises (something many of us love to do) but what New Year *actually* is, is the resetting of the calendar, isn't it? On New Year's day we start the year again as 1/1. That's what New Year *actually* is.

So how does this relate to us as hunter-gatherers?

If you've read "The Hunter-Gatherer Way" you'll know about Bernie Taylor's ideas from his book "Biological Time": that all the life cycles of animals, plants, fish, insects and humans are triggered by hormonal activity which is triggered by the changing amounts of lunar and solar light throughout the year.

When we were hunter-gatherers we had noticed that the Sun and the Moon are actually indicators as to where things are going to be and when. Which is a calendar.

Over thousands of years we built up our knowledge that if we mark the Sun's extremes at the two Solstice points (and we know when we've got to them because the sun rises from the same point for 3 or 4 mornings in a row) and the two Equinox points (when day and night are equal) and then note the *first full Moon* after each one, we will know exactly where everything we like to eat is going to be and when it will be there.

For example, the first full Moon after the Spring Equinox will trigger the oestrogen in wild geese so that they lay their eggs. This is why Easter is set as the first Sunday after the first full Moon after the Spring Equinox and Easter is the egg *hunt*.

So how does this all relate to New Year?

By noting the time lapse between the Winter Solstice and the first full Moon after it (which varies every year) we can see into the year ahead. A full Moon that falls 28 days after the Winter Solstice will mean the full Moon after the Spring Equinox will be a long time after it too and so spring will be late. And so on, throughout the whole year.

By marking the first full Moon after the Winter Solstice we can see the Natural calendar for the year ahead.

So just as Christmas was once the Winter Solstice celebration, I think New Year was once the celebration we had on the first full Moon after the Winter Solstice. From now on, I'm going to celebrate it then.

This is the hunter-gatherer way.

I went up to one of my special places on the high moor to make a fire and watch the full Moon rise, the first full Moon after the Winter Solstice.

As I walked there everything was very still and silent, no wind, no cloud movement and the birds were very obviously sitting quietly in the trees, facing East. Sometimes the small ones would lift off and then rearrange themselves but without any noise.

I became very aware of the reverence of the whole world around me, how I was walking into an *occasion* and how I was blundering in, my thoughts all over the place. The need to be socially aware in the wilderness is even more massive than in the hairdressers.

And I realised that every wild animal needed to be left alone at this point. Because *knowing* that this is the first full Moon after the Winter Solstice isn't what this is all about, this isn't just about re-setting our *knowledge* of the wild food calendar for the year ahead so we know where and when to find what we want, this is about re-setting our *own internal calendar.*

By *looking* at this Moon, its light triggers the receptors in our eyes so that our Pineal gland is stimulated to release certain hormones so that our biological calendar is re-set to fit in time with everything else's.

I am quite sure that every wild animal is doing this too.

I have often noticed the stillness and silence that comes with the rising of the full Moon and I've seen a whole flock of sheep standing facing it, all of them looking at it. And I've found my dog sitting on my bed just looking up at it too.

It's like how you would expect the holy night to feel: the silent night, the dear Christ enters in. In fact, the dear bright *Moon* enters in.

And every man and every beast stands side by side and watches and waits and becomes in time and in tune with each other.

This is the hunter-gatherer way.

I was thinking about how amazing it is that you can stir a teaspoonful of salt into a glass of water and the salt will completely disappear. How you can look into that glass and see nothing at all and not realize it's actually hiding a whole teaspoonful of salt.

And then I was thinking about how this happens in the air as well, how stuff just vanishes into the air. And how amazing it is that the two invisible substances that are around us - the air and the water - contain so many things, they are actually *cupboards*.

But the *stirring* is the key to it; stirring is the key to making things disappear. And so I was wondering whether there is something in Nature that causes the air and the water to be stirred so that these invisible realms can pick up and disappear all manner of things within them?

And I thought about how the wind and the tides, the high pressure to low pressure of the weather patterns, the turning of the Earth, the Sun and the Moon - what are they *actually doing?*

They are all contributing to *stirring* the air and the water so that the debris of life on Earth can be gathered up and cleaned and stored out of the way until it is needed again.

This is the hunter-gatherer way.

On several occasions recently while out for a walk in the woods or by the river, I've noticed that a Robin will fly quite close across my path and then land on a branch and look at me *very* intensely.

So, I have taken to turning over rocks, kicking rotten logs and digging in the leaf littered earth with the heel of my boot, then walking on.

And down will come the Robin in my wake, to pick out the food that Robin's like best.

This is the hunter-gatherer way.

This morning I taught a wild food walk in silence. Even I didn't speak a word.

I've wanted to try this for a long time, to take this final step into the unknown, and today's group were really keen to have a go.

Within a few moments of using gestures to convey what I wanted to say, I felt transported to the rainforest on a wild food walk I'd had with the Pygmy women when they had taught me like this because we'd had no other way to communicate. And I remembered how much we had laughed.

But, this mornings mimes were far from the subtle deftness of the Pygmy women, they began in very exaggerated gestures. For example, to convey that a plant could kill I drew a dramatic line across my neck and the others would respond with equally exaggerated expressions to show how afraid they were of it now.

But as the walk went on, I realised that just because these people weren't allowed to speak it didn't mean they were now blind as well. If anything, their eyesight was now heightened because they couldn't speak and so all I needed to do was to *slightly* shake my head and they would know this plant was poisonous. And their responses became more subtle too; the simplest response to realising a plant can kill is just a *slight* nod of the head.

When they realised a plant was edible, though, they jumped.

I found I couldn't move the group on to see the next plant until everyone had jumped. I realised that when this happened, a warm light seemed to shine over the whole group and then they were easy to move, as though they were actually hovering above the ground, and shining. But, if one person hadn't understood, the group could not easily be moved and I would have had to tug at it.

Some things were more difficult to mime than others - like trying to convey that you must check the underside of each Pennywort leaf because snails like to shelter there when it rains and if it's been a long shower they will stay there for some time and do their droppings there which you must check for them underneath and brush them off before you eat the leaf. One man understood my difficulty straight away and very gallantly stepped in to mime the part the others couldn't quite understand.

At the end, I asked how it had felt to receive this knowledge in gesture and mime. Everyone was unanimous in their love for it.

One man said he had found it instantly grounding; that it had taken him out of his intellect which he said would have wanted to ask masses of questions and offer up anecdotes, and instead had brought him straight into the present moment.

Silence had also heightened the senses of smell and touch and taste and perspective and colour and solemnity and delight and joy and wonder.

As we walked back the way we'd come, we were able to speak and I told them the names of each plant and tested them to see how much they had retained. They answered much more quickly than on the walks when

I had spoken and I realised this was because they didn't need to sift through all the things I'd said but went straight to their mental picture of it and the thoughts they'd had when they'd stored it there.

By being totally silent we had entered into the dimension of the present moment and instead of finding blank expressions and total misunderstandings there, we had instead found a whole language which we already knew and understood. And, after a bit of brushing up, we found that we loved that language.

This language, the "language of the present moment", does not come from the part of the mind with its need to constantly ask questions and share anecdotes.

The language of the present moment comes from when we were naturally without words, when we did not speak because we hadn't yet learned how. All of us know this language because all of us had already spent many months learning it, when we first arrived here. Using that language again as adults brought with it all the heightened senses and total joy of a being a baby.

This is the hunter-gatherer way.

Another completely silent wild food walk this morning, the silence only punctuated by the beautiful sound that people make when they suddenly understand. And bird by song. And nothing more.

We could have gone on like this forever; we did not want it to end. And where other spoken walks I've done have saturated the group by the 3/4 point, these people were not saturated at all, not even at the end.

I have never known a walk like it.

This is the hunter-gatherer way.

Very interesting feedback from someone who came on the completely silent Wild Food Walk:

"Hi Ffyona,

Thank you for the inspiring and magical foraging walk at the weekend. It was so great to do it without words getting in the way of the observing, and really I think we learnt a lot more and it was a lot clearer and easier that way.

I've been on a number of foraging walks but I think that your teaching style was probably the most accessible and clear that I've ever experienced in this field, partly because it's so simple. It was really enjoyable, thanks." Ben F

This is the hunter-gatherer way.

People share a lot of love after a wild food walk.

Maybe it's because wild food is the key to everything: ultimate health which cannot be found by eating anything else; absolute freedom: once you can feed yourself from Nature, you will never be a slave again; total and natural equality between the sexes and between people of all backgrounds; and the only way to unlock all of our physical, mental, emotional and spiritual abilities.

Or maybe it's because it just makes sense of our lives, and people really *love* that.

This is the hunter-gatherer way.

In these silent wild food walks, our messages are transmitted and understood in what feels like a substance in the air; it feels like we are surrounded and bound by the richest of sweet honeyed somethings.....

It has reminded me of what a Hopi Indian woman once told me as we washed our clothes in a launderette on the banks of the Rio Grande.

She said that many of the oldest Hopi stories begin with the line:

"Long, long ago, when people and animals spoke the same language...."

And suddenly I realised this was the language we'd used on the silent wild food walk.

This is the hunter-gatherer way.

It's not easy to get a group of people to understand the hunter-gatherer way when they are sitting down indoors listening to an evening talk.

If they were outside, Nature would seep into them and do the work for me but with four walls around them they become as separated from Nature as it's possible to be. And, from what I hear in the intellectual questions and statements that often follow a talk, separated from half of their brain too.

So, when asked to give a talk recently, I decided to do something about it. Time to apply "the spirit of exploration" and find a way through this, a way to make everyone *feel* as though they are outside even when they are not.

So, this is what I did:

I asked if I could do the talk by candlelight? And when that was okayed, I asked for the chairs to be arranged in a circle. Then I put the candles in the middle of the circle, lit them and turned out the light.

The effect was amazing, as though we were sitting around a campfire and it tricked our brains into thinking we were outside.

The feeling was pure magic. With not an intellect in sight.

This is the hunter-gatherer way.

I was invited up to Birmingham last week to give what I'd thought was going to be a talk about wild food. But when the taxi they'd arranged to meet me from the train station drove me into an abandoned industrial estate, I began to feel a little nervous.

Suddenly from behind a derelict facade, I found my hosts welcoming me into a beautiful vegetable garden they had created amongst the rubble and concrete.

A quick scan of the place and I soon realised that growing strongly from every crevice and scrap of earth it could find, was an abundance of wild food.

I chose Chickweed, Jack-by-the-Hedge, Red Dead Nettle, Wild Thyme, Ribwort Plantain and Landcress and laid them out on a mat by the fire for those who had gathered. I handed round little pieces for them to taste and they were simply amazed by the powerful flavours.

Then one man said "Where did you get these? They don't grow in Birmingham, you'd have to go a long way out of the city to find these."

And so I showed them how they were growing all around us and they could just reach out their hands and pick them.

They loved it. The fire was lit inside them. My job was done.

As I sat on the train home, I realised the irony of what had just happened: I noticed that my fee had been paid for by Birmingham University. And so a university had just paid me to teach people how to find wild food growing amongst the ruins of industry.

This is the hunter-gatherer way.

Watching a storm one evening last week, I noticed how the wind was moving the trees very differently depending on their kind: the Oaks were swaying their branches over their heads; the Horse Chestnuts were swinging them round their middles; and the Pines were heaving their shoulders up and down.

The wind, as invisible and as powerful as music, was dancing the trees, relaxing them in the way they liked best and ridding them of their stiff limbs.

No longer just a storm to me now, I think of it as a *party* for the trees.

And it went on until dawn.

This is the hunter-gatherer way.

I was thinking about this:

"Here we go gathering nuts in May" and how it just doesn't make any sense because there aren't any nuts in May.

But when something old like that doesn't make sense it's like a flag because I know it's saying "here there be lost knowledge" and I just have to find out what it is.

I don't believe that we used to fill our children's heads with nonsense like we do now, instead I think we took every opportunity we had to fill their heads with little tricks to help them remember what is really *important*.

The song "Here we go gathering nuts in May" gets stuck in your head and it repeats itself. It makes you want to skip. And swing a basket. And it makes you feel carefree and happy.

I think the song is to remind the children to go and look for the only nut that is ready in May: the Pignut. It's a delicious, fat, round tuber that grows deep in the earth and which children really, really love. They love to hunt for them, they love to dig for them and they love to eat them.

But, the Pignut plant can be easily confused with other umbellifers whose roots are deadly poisonous so it would make sense that the game that goes with the song is about choosing *others* to go with them.

This is the hunter-gatherer way.

A group of mothers and small children from an inner-city area came on a Seaweed Wild Food Walk with me. Some of the children had never been to the shore before.

So they carried on as though they were in the city and they screamed and tugged and tantrumed their way over the sand, demanding that the wind be stopped, and the sea be stopped, and the sand be stopped.

The mothers shouted and tugged and scolded even more loudly after them.

And so I gave up the idea of giving out any meaningful information about which seaweeds were good to eat. Instead I just watched for the moment when Nature would rein everyone in and absorb them into wonder.

The moment came when one of the girls said she had seen a fish in a rock pool. Suddenly, as if by magic, all the children instinctively gathered on the edge of the pool and peered in. They were all quiet for the first time and they were all in the same stance and they were all in the same mind.

This little fish, no bigger than a matchstick, had gathered in the children and the mothers and united them.

And when it flicked its tail, and everyone saw it, they all made the most beautiful sound of "Oooh!" And the music of it poured out over the water and fell into it and I think the little fish must have heard it and felt it; an overwhelming expression of awe and wonder in its being.

From then on the children behaved very differently: they wanted to hold each others hands now, they wanted to help each other and so they tackled a great rocky embankment like the mighty and wondrous tribe they really are.

Thank you dear little fish, you changed their lives forever.

This is the hunter-gatherer way.

"The Saga of the Portland Sago"

I had read somewhere that the roots of the poisonous Arum Lilly were used during the War to make a milk pudding called "Portland Sago".

But, I never wanted to try and make it myself because when I was first learning the wild food of spring I had accidently poisoned myself by eating an Arum Lilly leaf instead of a *Sorrel* leaf. They look very similar to the untrained eye and my tongue had been burned and blistered and swelled up so much that it prized my mouth open and I couldn't speak for about 4 hours. I couldn't phone for help because all I could do was make spluttering noises.

In the weeks afterwards I studiously applied myself to finding the consistent and reliable differences between the two plants so that I would never make the same mistake again.

And now, after many years of successfully identifying and eating Sorrel, I decided to challenge myself to making friends with the Arum Lilly again and making Portland Sago from its root.

I began by looking for a recipe for the milk pudding on-line. So many people are experimenting with wild food now and I was sure that someone would have worked it out. But, I found nothing. The only references I could find to it were that it was made during the War as a milk pudding substitute when Sago couldn't be had.

But different books said such different things for the preparation of it: some said the roots must be soaked for a month first; others that just baking them and pounding them would make the pudding. It was all far too vague to be an account of what someone had *actually* done and so I didn't trust any of it.

So, I had come to a dead-end.

I recognised it was a dead-end because absolutely *nothing* was furthering the quest after two days of searching. I knew that if I left it there I would feel deeply unsatisfied and I really didn't want to go back to my Year Long Wild Food course students saying that I couldn't find the answer and we'd all sit around looking glum and feeling dead-endish and beaten.

I couldn't bear to see faces like that.

So, I went back to the beginning of the mystery and carefully looked at each element: *Portland Sago was the term given to a milk pudding made from the roots of Arum Lilly during the War when they couldn't get hold of Sago.* So, which part of that can I explore to find out more?

What about the word "Portland"? Why was it called that?

I looked up "Portland" and found there is an island of Portland off the Dorset coast. I then looked up to see if the island had a tourist information office and found that it did. So, I rang them and asked if they knew anything about a thing called Portland Sago. They said "Yes." And went on to tell me the story.

They said that during the Second World War a call went out to the nation to find a source of starch from a non-food source. A woman called Mrs Gibbs from the Portland Arms had answered the call by remembering that it had once been obtained from Arum Lilly roots. So, in honour of her it was always referred to as "Portland Sago".

"Great!" I said, "Can you give me the recipe as I'd like to have a go at making it?" I imagined them saying they even had a commemorative booklet full of black and white photos of women in the War gathering the roots and making the pudding, with a photo of Mrs Gibbs handwritten recipe at the back.

"No, sorry. We don't have the recipe unfortunately."

What? That didn't make any sense.

"Sorry."

Back to the drawing board.

I looked more closely at this new piece of information: *a call went out to the nation to find a new source of starch from a non-food source.*

Why?

Why did they need starch in the first place?

Because, you might think, you need starch in your diet because so many people are now fighting they need more carbohydrates. But, it was starch from a *non-food* source. Which probably meant it was *not* for food.

What would they need non-food starch for in a War?

What is starch *actually* used for?

What is it used for in *my* life? My Mother always starched our napkins, she put them in a solution of starch after washing them and it made them stiff. When I was a young child at boarding school, our shirts were always starched by the laundry, they would come back so firmly stuck together you had to force your hand down through the sleeves to prize the sides apart.

What is there about starch in our culture?

Nurses always had starched white aprons.

Why do it? Why starch the aprons? Why starch the napkins? Why starch the shirts of children in an institution?

What does starch *do* to cotton fabric?

I looked it up and found that starch fills in the gaps in the weave of the fabric so that whatever hits the fabric will not *stain* it.

Why would a war need fabric that does not stain?

Because in a war there is an awful lot of blood.

And nurses with aprons covered in bloody stains wouldn't do at all.

So, the thinking must have been: There is going to be a war, we will need starch. Where do we get starch from at the moment? From maize which is a food source. We need all the food we can get so we must get starch from a non-food source. How do we do that? Don't know. But somebody out there will have the answer. Let's put out a call to the nation for someone to come up with starch from a non-food source.

And Mrs Gibbs from the Portland Arms remembered that in Tudor times, the great concertinaed collars of Lords and Ladies were stiffened with the starch from the roots of Arum Lilies. Which is probably why it's also called Lords and Ladies.

A process would have been worked out so that the people who extracted the starch from the roots didn't get blistered hands like the launderers of old and the resulting greyish-white pulp looked so much like a milk pudding that it was given the name of "Portland *Sago*".

It would have killed me if I'd eaten it.

And some people think that recovering lost wild food knowledge is easy.

There is a cupboard under the Crab Apple tree which I never noticed before.

I was visiting a tree that always has fruit longer than any of the others but I found no fruit at all. There were none on its bare branches and the earth beneath the tree was just strewn with dry leaves where the fallen Crabs should be.

I couldn't believe it, I thought they couldn't all have gone so quickly. I thought I must just see if there were any that had fallen and had been covered by the leaves and so I pulled away a few here and there.

Soon I'd found a whole collection of the little golden apples neatly tucked into the soft mud.

They were all standing the right way up with their little stalks at the top and packed about by the soft earth so that only a small golden circle of them was showing.

Does this always happen? I wondered. And I thought of all the other Crab Apple trees I know and how they all have such soft mud at their base. So soft is this mud that the little apples are always sinking into it and giving me the yucky job of pulling them out.

And I thought of how clever this is for the little animals who like them: they don't have to drag them or roll them, the apples are stored neatly where they fall. A little animal with its nose close to the ground will soon know which pile of leaves to clear away with its paws to reveal an apple. And then I thought of all the other cupboards of wild fruit that must be in the Earth right now and how the dry leaves that are blown from the trees cover them over, like closing their little doors. All tucked in, all ready for winter.

This is the hunter-gatherer way.

I noticed that Elsa had started to lag a bit whilst helping me to make the fantastically abundant numbers of Wild Food Identification booklets that had been ordered for Christmas presents.

She had decided to spend her earnings on getting new winter rugs for her horse but she was getting very tired and still had so many more to make before she reached her goal.

I knew she needed something immediate to revive her interest and so I just watched her for a moment to see if something would come. I watched her folding the pages of coloured illustrations and binding them together with raffia and putting them in the envelopes addressed to the four corners of the country.

And I suddenly realised that these aren't just *Wild Food Identification booklets*, they are the culmination of all the adventures she and I have shared over the last 15 years as she grew up learning the wild food of the moors and valleys and seashore as we unearthed the long forgotten knowledge.

So I said: "These aren't just identification booklets you know, they're actually *adventure* books! And we're sending them all over the country so that other people can have the adventures we did!"

She suddenly lit up like a Christmas tree, and turned with a new will to her task. It was so beautiful to behold; a young person sharing the wealth of what she has loved.

This is the hunter-gatherer way.

Whilst watching hundreds of people visit my wild food market stalls over Christmas, I saw a pattern of behaviour where the adults would be unable to solve the puzzle I set for them but the children would get it straight away.

The puzzle was that I would offer the visitors a taste of my wild food chocolate mousse but they would have to guess the wild ingredient.

The adults would take a teaspoonful, lift their eyes away from the stall and concentrate on the flavours. When they couldn't identify the wild ingredient they would look back at me and say they just couldn't guess.

The children, on the other hand, would ask "Is it *seaweed*?" And their parents would be *amazed*.

So, I began watching what the children were doing that their parents weren't. They would take a teaspoonful, continue to look at me whilst concentrating on the flavours, realise they couldn't identify the wild ingredient and then look on the stall for *clues*.

Right in front of them were rows and rows of packages that said: "Seaweed Chocolate Mousse Pack".

Somewhere in our modern education we are taught not to look for clues anymore, it makes us think that most of life's mysteries are beyond the possibility of our understanding and we give up on them.

But when we were children, we still had the sense to know that the answers to life's mysteries are often right in front of us.

This is the hunter-gatherer way.

As I was running last night under the stars, heading straight for the Plough, I was thinking about my old saying that "If I can see the stars then the stars can see me".

This time I had another thought: "But they can't see me because I am in the dark and I carry no light of my own".

And then I thought that the stars can only see the Earth when the Sun shines upon it.

And when the Sun goes, the Earth disappears.

So the Earth must look like it's flashing.

And I thought how similar that is to a lighthouse.

But a lighthouse is turning, beaming out its light as it goes.

And then I remembered that the Earth is turning too, and so it must be beaming out its light like a lighthouse as it goes.

Sunlight is at its richest at the Winter Solstice.

It is the most golden in colour and as it pours out over the landscape at dawn and dusk it seems to move more slowly as though it is thicker than at any other time of the year.

Elsa once called it a "cordial of light".

There isn't very much of it but then, like all cordials, if we had too much of it we would be sick.

This is the hunter-gatherer way.

Another night I was running, it was the first full Moon after the Winter Solstice and it had been the first warm day of the year. As I passed the dark row of hedges I realised I could smell the plants for the first time in weeks.

Warmed by the winter Sun that day they had awakened and so each plant was releasing its scent. It was as though this smell was the plant's song. A song that was saying "I am a Hawthorn tree and I am alive!"

This is the hunter-gatherer way.

I'm still fascinated by the idea that a glass of clear water can hide things that you have stirred into it. You can look at it, this invisible substance, and never know there was a teaspoonful of salt in there. It has completely disappeared.

What else is in there? If you want to find out you have to apply stillness and it will reveal what it was hiding.

How air can contain so many things that the wind has stirred into it: huge amounts of pollen; tonnes of mushrooms spores; dust; and all manner of things that have completely vanished inside the air. To get them out you also have to apply stillness.

Apart from air and water, are there any other invisible substances?

How about music? It's so very powerful and yet completely invisible. And I think it can hide things too. I think this because for a time I was listening to a piece of guitar music over and over and over again and as I did so I got the sudden urge to start drawing. Out came a holly leaf.

I continued drawing as I listened and I filled a notebook full of plants and flowers.

Later, I found out that the musician I was listening to, Alex Knight, likes to play his guitar by the river and out in the woods and up on the moor and I think that maybe, while he was playing, elements of Nature fell into his music and I heard them and drew them out.

This is the hunter-gatherer way.

As the spring plants are emerging, I remember having lunch with Clio Wondrousch, the woman who, many years ago, had taught me some of its wild foods.

She had put sheepskins on the floor in front of the wood burning stove and had boiled eggs for us. She'd grated wild horseradish root and mixed it with clotted cream and she'd pounded wild garlic leaves with rock salt and oil. I had just *loved* watching her do all of this.

To this I had added a loaf of rye bread and the "Salad that Sings", a mixture of the 15 wild leaves and flowers she'd taught me.

We'd feasted. We'd laughed. We'd shared stories of wild food walks we've taught. And I was so pleased to tell her how I have begun each walk with one of her blessings, said in a circle while holding hands. And then remaining silent throughout the walk until we gather in another circle to say the blessing again.

She was pleased to hear this and that because of the silence, all we can hear, instead of an insatiable series of questions, is Mother Nature giving us the answers.

This is the hunter-gatherer way.

I love it when people add a new piece to the "Ring of the Wild Food Year" by making connections.

Elsa is studying for her Biology GCSE and she suddenly realised *why* most of the spring wild foods are so fiery hot in flavour.

She'd often heard me say that the spring greens raise our metabolism but that I didn't know how and she'd just read that it's *heat* that stimulates our enzymes to raise the metabolism.

So, she put two and two together and realised the effect of the fiery flavours is to raise our metabolism, which makes perfect sense. Clever girl.

This is the hunter-gatherer way.

Like all animals I have known, when my dog is happy she emits a lovely sweet smell. But I've just noticed that it is very strong around her paws.

It makes me think that other animals could be emitting the smell of their emotional state through their paws too.

This would make sense because then the smell would be left in their footprints for predators, or lovers, to interpret and follow.

And so to an animal, footpaths through the woods must be like a rainbow of emotion.

This is the hunter-gatherer way.

I noticed that a beautiful thing has happened when I recognise an edible wild plant in the hedgerow: I no longer hear its name in my head as I once did.

Instead, I get the taste of it in my mouth.

It's like a greeting.

It's like a kiss.

This is the hunter-gatherer way.

These days I have taken to gathering the spring wild food without a basket. Instead I make a bunch of it in my hand. It means I can run as I gather, which I do now a lot, because it makes me feel so good.

Looking at this bunch of edible blue/green leaves and pink, yellow and white flowers in my hand, I realise it looks just like a posy.

And I think of how we once were: living simply in a landscape of oak and beech and water-meadows with barefooted children running home to their cave on tiny animal trails proudly holding pretty posies of wild flowers in their hands, for their lunch.

This is the hunter-gatherer way.

Just recently I noticed there's some very special magic in something quite ordinary. It happened when I was watching a small snail stretching up its eyestalks exploring a leaf above it. I thought: wouldn't it be interesting to see if I can look into the eye of this snail?

I have often enjoyed looking into the eye of a Robin or a deer or a rabbit. To do it I just concentrate my focus on where their eye should be, no matter how far away they are, until it becomes distinctive and then I can see the animal's expression in the light of its eyes.

But, a snail's eye is so much smaller. Could I really make it big enough to see?

As I concentrated on that tiny dot, everything else began to blur around it and soon the eye was growing bigger and bigger in front of me and when it was so big that it completely filled my vision, I looked into it. And the snail was looking back at me.

It was giving me the kind of look you would expect from an easy-going garden snail who is curious about who is saying hello to it. As we just looked at each other, I felt myself being filled up with its sweetness and gentleness.

After a little while I started to relax my focus, allowing the rest of the snail to come back into view and then the leaf and then the flowers and then the whole hedge.

And when I looked for the snail again to see how it felt about things now, it was so small I could hardly find it and when I looked for its eye again it was far too tiny to make out at all.

This is the hunter-gatherer way.

I am so very proud of the work my students on the Year Long Wild Food course have been doing.

One of them, Flora Arbuthnott, has just led her first walk for the Bristol Food Festival and chose to teach her group in silence, just as I taught her and just as the Pygmies in the Zaire rainforest taught me, all those years ago.

I have no words to describe how good this feels.

This is the hunter-gatherer way.

I was looking at the flaming bright flowers on a gorse bush up on the moor and felt the most overwhelming feeling that they simply *love* being gorse flowers.

I wondered what reaction I would get if I looked at anything else and asked it if it loved being itself? And this is what I found:

Dandelions *love* being Dandelions

Butterflies *love* being Butterflies

Skylarks *love* being Skylarks

Pink ears on lambs *love* being pink ears on lambs

Stones *love* being stones

The wind *loves* being the wind

Sunlight *loves* being sunlight

But, oil doesn't seem to feel the same way about being a crisp packet.

And then I asked it of myself.

And it was the single most helpful question I think I have ever asked myself.

It instantly shed me of all that I am cloaked in and encased by, enabling me to feel instantly free, to feel strong and healthy and alive.

Yes, I *love* being me.

Just being me, happily, makes this moment perfect.

This is the hunter-gatherer way.

The world has turned into flowers: Bluebells and yellow Primroses, Red Campion and white Stitchwort.

Swathes of green garlic leaves have become galaxies of white stars; Jack-by-the-hedge has produced its snowy crown; and what was recently just an empty green meadow is now festooned with golden Dandelions and Buttercups and pink tipped Daisies.

Hawthorn trees have turned into giant posies in pink or white; and the vast branches of Horse Chestnut trees seem almost held up by their great candle stacks of white flowers.

The world no longer has need of our services to do the job of pruning and thinning out the leaves and the roots.

What the world needs now are the insects to do the next job for it: pollination.

And the warm moist weather that brings out the insects, and the bites and the stings and the buzzings they bring in the still muggy air are *hell* for us.

So, we leave for the best place in the world for us now: the vast open horizons of the ocean shore. And here the sea breezes have cleared the air of insects and we find we have a new job to do: this time to prune and thin out the seaweed and the seashore plants and the fish.

And when these jobs are done in the early autumn and the seashore plants turn to seed and the seaweeds break off in the storms and the fish swim away, we start getting cold in the damp air as it sinks.

And so will head inland to the world we are leaving now to find that the insects have turned it into a land of wild nuts and seeds and fruits and we are welcomed back with open arms.

Because everything needs us to do a job for it again.

This is the hunter-gatherer way.

Eating wild food means feeding yourself with love.

There is love in the adventure of exploring; there is love in the spark of joy at the finding; there is love in the moment of gathering; and there is *heavenly bliss* in the eating.

This is the hunter-gatherer way.

My ritual when I wake up in the morning is to make a cup of tea and take it back to bed with me, light a candle, get comfy and say a meta meditation to align myself with my core again after the adventures of my dreams.

The meditation goes like this:

May I live in safety
May I have happiness in my body
May I have happiness in my mind
May I have ease of well-being

But recently I have noticed that I don't need to say the meditation anymore because everything I have been trying to *feel* by saying it is actually happening much more profoundly in the tea cup itself.

In my dark blue hand-thrown tea cup I can see all of this happening as the beautiful spirals of steam from the hot water curl upwards into the cold air.

The water is demonstrating what it *really* means to live in safety because it is completely free to change from one form to another.

All you have to do to feel this within you is to look into the curls of the rising steam and imagine yourself within them, stretching your body like them, delighting in your mind like them, moving with the ease of them.

You can carry this feeling with you throughout your day and if you need a top up you can always do it by staring at the steam rising from someone else's teacup.

This is the hunter-gatherer way.

When we gather wild food we are stimulating the plant into action, like a lamb head butting a teat to produce more milk.

This is the hunter-gatherer way.

Did you know that trees not only transform carbon dioxide into oxygen, they also transform sadness and despair into comfort and love?

To experience this for yourself all you have to do is to find the biggest tree you can, stand underneath it and then look up into its great branches full of leaves and sunlight.

Tell the tree all your troubles. And when you have finished put your arms around its trunk.

You'll feel better then.

This is the hunter-gatherer way.

I had a dream last night that I was a Blue Whale. A giant of muscle. I was asking myself "Where can I go for a massage?"

I realised that the only place on Earth that is strong enough to give me a massage is the pressure of the water in the depths of the ocean.

So, I swam down there, up and down, up and down, getting all the knots out.

Scientists don't know why whales and Great White sharks swim down to the bottom of the ocean but I think I do.

This is the hunter-gatherer way.

In the midst of going through a crisis in the last 6 weeks, my daughter, Elsa, gave me the most beautiful hug and said:

"Why don't you just go for a wild food walk Mum? You'll feel better then."

This was absolutely the *last* thing on my mind but the love in her voice spoke so powerfully to me that I just took her advice and went.

Within a few hundred yards of walking amongst the wild food on the seashore, I felt myself being lifted up and out of blackness and into a paradise of purple and butterflies and joy.

Everything was gleaming with an inner light so powerful and delighting in itself for being alive and so unaffected by those that were contributing to the darkening of my own light, that I realised that Nature is bigger than anyone.

And that's what I needed to know: that something was bigger than the person who was trying to overwhelm me.

When I returned home I felt so empowered that I was able to see through the impossible situation and navigate my way through to a successful outcome.

This is the hunter-gatherer way.

I was just playing with my dog, Cara, on the sheepskin by the fire. Suddenly I realised that a state of love was holding us within it.

Holding us within it.

Like water holding salt.

And suddenly it felt like this state was affecting all the possibilities of my life, that they were now opening up into vastness, as though anything could drop out of it and into our laps and onto our paths.

Love, like water, is an invisible force. I think it is the substance that holds all that we need. To get the love to release those things, we just need to abandon ourselves to the moment we are sharing with another.

This is the hunter-gatherer way.

Thanks to the dedicated clean up efforts of local people and businesses and the council, a salt water estuary has begun to attract wildlife again.

For the first time in many years Otters have been seen in the area, joyfully feeding on the incoming tide. And early this morning, just before sunrise, a hunter-gatherer was seen, perhaps for the first time in 2,000 years, feeding on long forgotten delicacies.

It was heaven.

This is the hunter-gatherer way.

My reward for finishing a section of this book was to go and explore a line of Blackthorn trees I'd recently been surprised by.

I'd been surprised by them because of how large and ripe their Sloes are for this time of year and I wanted to see if I could gather them before anyone else does.

As I walked along, scanning each of the trees to see which had fruit, I wondered whether it's OK to gather the berries now? Because even though they look ripe, I don't normally gather them till October.

Then a beautiful song came to mind and I found myself singing it every time I found berries. It felt like the pleasure of finding them was just welling up inside me and pouring itself out in a beautiful greeting for the love of them and I felt myself walking and singing sweetly as if in a honey pool with the trees.

But, the first time I tried to gather the fruit the tree wouldn't let go of it. I pulled the Sloe and the whole tree came with it. I let go and the tree flung itself backwards very dramatically and then re-arranged itself with a lot of rustling. I apologised.

The next tree I came to had berries and they were just as beautifully purple as the first but this time, pulling very gently to see if it was OK, the berry came away easily.

Why would that be?

And as I walked along, singing to each new tree and trying to gather its berries, I realised that even though the Sloes all look the same, the colour of the *leaves* is the clue to their ripeness:

The Blackthorn trees whose leaves are *green* won't give you their fruit, no matter how hard you pull.

But, the trees whose leaves are *brown* and falling, will.

And then I noticed the song I'd been singing all along: it was the Greg Lake song C'est la Vie. And the part I was singing was this:

"C'est la vie,
Have your leaves all turned to brown?
Have you scattered them around you?
C'est la vie."

Perhaps they weren't just a beautiful greeting for the love of the fruit but had come to mind from the tree itself to tell me what I must look for:

"Blackthorn tree,
Have your leaves all turned to brown?
Have you scattered them around you?
Blackthorn tree."

This is the hunter-gatherer way.

There aren't many wild animals left in Britain to hunt. I noticed the same thing in the Australian outback when hunting with the Aborigines. They said the animals have all left. They said they will come back when the white man leaves.

Same as in Britain. When the male ego leaves.

I don't think the ego can get out of control when a man is hunting for food for his family. He is disciplined by Nature then.

This is the hunter-gatherer way.

It's raining so heavily outside and I'm all cosy and warm and feeling good and I'm thinking: what is this rain *actually* doing?

After the long, long golden dry autumn, Nature is finally taking over the land that we played in and decomposing it back into its constituent parts.

With this rain the leaves and bodies and branches and uneaten fruits can begin to melt into the earth and the mycelium that runs through the soil can be activated to break down the cells walls of the decomposing matter to release the elements inside.

After all the fun we had, this rain is Mother Nature running through the playroom and dismantling the games we all made back into their separate boxes, so that they are ready to be used for next time.

This is the hunter-gatherer way.

One Halloween the leaves were still on the trees and they were still green.

Why would that be?

People will blame it on global warming but I don't think it's that (though I do believe in global warming).

Seasonal changes are triggered by light, both lunar and solar.

This year the Full Moon was almost as late as it can be after the Autumn Equinox which is what has set everything back. So rather than fixing Halloween as a date in the modern calendar, I think the true date is actually the second full Moon after the Autumn Equinox.

Every year, no matter when this Moon falls, the leaves will always be bright orange and the trunks of the trees will always be black. These are the colours of Halloween, the closing of the door on the gathering in and the beginning of two months of snuggling.

This is the hunter-gatherer way.

Walking through the woods early one damp morning and I could see wood smoke hanging heavily in the valley below.

I longed to catch its sweet scent because wood smoke so completes the earthy damp smell of the dawn that it makes everything seem right with the world.

But, not everyone's fire smells good of course.

It made me think what an important question that is to keep in mind as we go through our day: how sweet is the smoke of my fire?

This is the hunter-gatherer way.

When you notice the work of sunlight: like the pattern it makes on the surface of the river and then reflects that up onto the underside of a tree branch, like a moving animal skin; or when a leaf gleams that intense florescent yellow with the sunlight just pouring through it; or when you walk along a hedge and the sunlight catches at the corner of your eye and blasts it with what first feels like a blinding flash but then as you get used to it you see the flashes are actually giving you glimpses of another dimension; and then stand at the top of a hill as the Sun sets and tell it where you saw its beautiful work that day, you are doing something very important.

This came from standing on the top of a hill and watching the Sun rise one morning through a layer of thick, brown crud and thinking it looked so old and forgotten and unappreciated.

This is the hunter-gatherer way.

For years I marvelled at how completely camouflaged the wild mushrooms are in their environment. But after 28 years of mushroom hunting I don't think like that now.

As soon as I see yellow Silver Birch leaves on green grass I instantly think "Chanterelles!" because the fallen Silver Birch leaves are the same size and shape and colour as these delicious mushrooms which often grow amongst them.

As soon as I see that particular yellow/green combination it has the effect of making me stop and scan each leaf carefully for the tell tale signs that it is actually a mushroom.

So, in reality, the Chanterelles' similarity to the leaves where they grow doesn't work like camouflage at all, it works in exactly the opposite way as *advertising*.

I think the mushrooms are the same colour and size and shape as the leaves they grow amongst not so that you *don't* see them but so that you *do*.

This is the hunter-gatherer way.

Sometimes, when I'm feeling low, I go to the woods just to look for diamonds. I find them dancing on the surface of the streams, or gleaming at me from drops of dew in the grass or sparkling through the leaves.

And the world feels like a better place again.

This is the hunter-gatherer way.

If you want to think differently just take off your shoes.

Turn them upside down and look at the pattern of wear on the soles. You might see that the heel of one foot is more worn than the heel of other and that the ball of the opposite one is more worn too. Now try walking by putting the unworn heel down first and rolling harder on the other ball.

Do this for 20 strides and you'll think differently.

This is the hunter-gatherer way.

The only time I was able to get out a few days ago was at dusk. I wondered whether I would be able to find any wild mushrooms up on the high moor and if so, whether their colours would have changed in the twilight.

I always know where I am up there but if I ever get confused all I'd have to do is to keep walking downhill to find a stream and follow that down to civilisation.

In the purple-pink light of the gloaming, the grass still glowed green and sure enough, I could easily make out a sprinkling of pale orangey Meadow Wax Cap mushrooms shining out like beacons.

I gathered some into my basket and, humming gently (the Stranglers song, "Golden Brown"), I followed their trail across the moor, upwards into the advancing mist.

The wind blew the Moon free and her warm silver presence cast a quiet magic upon everything, reassuring and loving and I drank deeply from the wonder of where I was.

As I did so, I realised that despite the mist, my hair, my skin and my woollen jumper were completely dry: the wind must have been stronger than the water it carried.

And when all the colours began merging as one, I felt the door was closing for the night and I turned for home and hearth to cook these wondrous gifts and feel the lifting of my spirits into even higher realms.

This is the hunter-gatherer way.

SURVIVAL INTERNATIONAL

Survival International is the only charity campaigning for the rights of tribal peoples worldwide.

Survival was founded in 1969 in response to the secret genocide of Amazonian Indians. Over the last 40 years Survival has campaigned relentlessly for tribal lives and lands, and to permanently eradicate racist misconceptions.

From the Guarani in Brazil, to the Bushmen in Botswana, tribal peoples all over the world are under threat from material and cultural 'progress'.

Please help us to ensure a future for these highly diverse and intricate peoples. Visit the Survival website www.survivalinternational.org and find out more about their current campaigns.

Please also consider giving to Survival. Survival refuses government funding which means it relies on its supporters for everything it does. Your contribution, however small, will allow them to help tribal peoples gain the respect and equality that is rightfully theirs in the 21st century.

Thank you,

Ffyona Campbell

AN AFTER THOUGHT AT THE END OF CHAPTER 3

I knew there must be more to it than just awe and wonder; I knew there had to be a practical reason for bringing down lightning but I just couldn't think what it might be. And then, a couple of weeks after I'd sent the manuscript to the printers, something made sense:

The person who had sat in the stone circle during a storm and had seen a wall get smashed in two by a lightning bolt was the clue.

I looked up information about the power of lightning and found an article in the National Geographic Magazine:

(news.nationalgeographic.com/news/2014/01/140105-lightning-mountains-south-africa-drakensberg-mountains-geology).

It says that until now no one suspected that lightning is a major sculptor of mountains. The way it works is explained by geologist Jasper Knight from Johannesburg's University of the Witwatersrand who says that lightning heats up water inside the rock so fast "It basically causes a bomb to explode on the rock surface,"

Why would the Bronze Age elite be interested in doing that? Because the Bronze Age elite wanted *metal*. I therefore think they were drawing down the lightning in order to blast the rock for mining.

Awe and wonder was just the very useful by-product.